Justyna's Narrative

4/97

5

Justyna's Narrative

-➤-◄-

Gusta Davidson Draenger

EDITED WITH
AN INTRODUCTION BY
Eli Pfefferkorn and David H. Hirsch

TRANSLATED BY
Roslyn Hirsch and David H. Hirsch

The University of Massachusetts Press
AMHERST

*The manuscript of Gusta Davidson Draenger and
the Introduction to the Polish Edition were originally published in
Polish as* Pamientnik Justyny, 1946, *The Jewish Historical Commission
of the Central Committee of Polish Jews — Krakow, Poland.
The English translation is published by the University of
Massachusetts Press in cooperation with
Beit Lohamei Haghetaot, Israel.*

→>—<←

New material copyright © 1996
by the University of Massachusetts Press

LC 96–734
ISBN 1–55849–037–X (cloth); 038–8 (pbk.)

Designed by Steve Dyer
Set in Sabon by Keystone Typesetting, Inc.
Printed and bound by Thomson-Shore

LIBRARY OF CONGRESS CATALOGING-IN-PUBLICATION DATA
Justyna, 1917 or 18–1943.
[Pamietnik Justyny. English]
Justyna's narrative / Gusta Davidson Draenger ; edited with an
introduction by Eli Pfefferkorn and David H. Hirsch ; translated by
Roslyn Hirsch and David H. Hirsch.
p. cm.
Includes bibliographical references.
ISBN 1–55849–037–X (cloth : alk. paper).
— ISBN 1–55849–038–8 (pbk. : alk. paper)
1. Justyna, 1917 or 18–1943.
2. Holocaust, Jewish (1939–1945) — Poland — Kraków — Personal narratives.
3. Jews — Poland — Kraków — Persecutions.
4. World War, 1939–1945 — Jewish resistance — Poland — Kraków.
5. World War, 1939–1945 — Prisoners and prisons, German.
I. Pfefferkorn, Eli.   II. Hirsch, David H.   III. Hirsch, Roslyn.   IV. Title.
IN PROCESS
940.53′18′094386 — dc20   96–734
CIP

British Library Cataloguing in Publication data are available.

Contents

+>-<+

entnik Justyny had never been published in English. After establishing contact with surviving members of the Akiba underground, he interviewed them in Israel in October 1987; sections of these interviews are included in the Editors' Introduction. He then asked us whether we would be interested in translating the *Pamientnik*. We began right away.

After we had finished translating the published Polish version, Pfefferkorn arranged for historian Israel Gutman to deliver into our hands another fifteen pages of typescript, transcriptions of original scraps from the archive of the Ghetto Fighters Kibbutz in Israel. This material has never before been published in any language. Our translation of these lyrical pages forms the opening of this English text, under the headings "Justyna's Last Will and Testament" and "Kopaliny." The new materials give fuller expression to Draenger's romantic idealism and to the ideological proclivities of the Akiba Youth Movement.

In his study of Jewish resistance movements in World War II, Joseph Tenenbaum writes that *Pamientnik Justyny* "remains the most moving, the most captivating narrative that has come out of these terrible times. No account of partisan movements can afford to omit it." We hope our translation comes close to doing justice to this unexpected eruption of grandeur from the cauldron of degradation that was the Holocaust. Having spent nearly four years of her childhood in ghettos and in hiding from the Nazis, Roslyn wishes to express her admiration for those courageous souls who fought to preserve the human dignity of us all.

ROSLYN HIRSCH
DAVID H. HIRSCH

Acknowledgments

➤➤◄◄

A project of this kind is rarely achieved without incurring more debts than the authors can possibly acknowledge. Among those who deserve special thanks are Judy Lachman, who supported the project both morally and financially, and Hela Rufeisen-Schipper, who was not only one of the primary actors in the events detailed in *Justyna's Narrative,* but who also helped smooth the way for the translators and editors, as did Yehuda Maimon. Kay Ackerman assisted Eli Pfefferkorn in conducting interviews with survivors of the Akiba underground in Israel. Vered Pfefferkorn transcribed the interviews and translated much of the interview material from Hebrew to English. We are grateful to Roman Weingarten and the New Cracow Friendship Society and the archive of Kibbutz Lohamei Haghetaot for their cooperation. Professor Daniel Grinberg of the Jewish Historical Institute of Warsaw was kind enough to send us important materials in Polish and Yiddish from the ZIH archive. Vicki Caron read the translation at an early stage and gave many useful suggestions, as did Nessa Olshansky-Ashtar. Our editor Janet Benton's careful attention to detail and her probing questions improved the translation and helped shed light on textual puzzles. We would also like to thank Bryan Shepp, Dean of the College of Brown University, and Ernest Frerichs, chair of the Program in Judaic Studies, for providing financial support from research funds.

A Brief Chronology
of the Krakow Ghetto

→►◄←

SEPTEMBER 1, 1939: Germans invade Poland

SEPTEMBER 6, 1939: Germans in Krakow

OCTOBER 12, 1939: *Generalgouvernment* installed, with Krakow as capital

DECEMBER 1939: *Judenrat* formed, 24 members, with Mark Bieberstein as chair

MAY 18 TO AUGUST 15, 1940: Jews still permitted to leave city of Krakow

SUMMER 1940: *Jüdischer Ordnungsdienst* formed (Jewish ghetto police)

MARCH 21, 1941: Krakow Ghetto comes into being

JUNE 22, 1941: Germans invade U.S.S.R.

DECEMBER 1941: Akiba Youth Movement sets up farm in Kopaliny

JUNE 1, 1942: *Aktion Reinhard* — 2,000 Jews deported to Belzec, and several hundred resisters shot on the spot

JUNE 3–4, 1942: Germans return to ghetto. By June 6, about 5,000 people deported to Belzec or murdered in ghetto

MID-1942: Hashomer Hatzair and Akiba start underground resistance

AUGUST 1942: Farm in Kopaliny abandoned

SEPTEMBER TO OCTOBER 1942: Joint command of Jewish Fighting Organization set up

SEPTEMBER 20, 1942: First group of five moves into forest

OCTOBER 1942: Plaszow camp founded; it held 2,000 Jews when S.S.

Untersturmfuehrer (Second Lieutenant) Amon Leopold Goeth took over in February 1943

OCTOBER 28, 1942: Second *aktzia* in ghetto — 6,000 Jews deported, several hundred murdered on the spot

NOVEMBER 20, 1942: "The Last Supper"

DECEMBER 22, 1942: Attack on Cyganeria Cafe

DECEMBER 24, 1942: Dolek Liebeskind killed

JANUARY 1943: Szymek Draenger arrested

FEBRUARY 1943: Ghetto divided by barbed wire into two compounds

Surviving Jews segregated into skilled workers and technicians, who with their families numbered some 10,000, and "nonproductive Jews, who numbered over 4,000. The first were imprisoned in 'A' Ghetto, from where they daily set out to work in various factories and workshops . . ., while the second were imprisoned in 'B' Ghetto, where they starved and lived in a state of constant terror . . ." (Ainsztein 1974, 826).

FEBRUARY 1943: Goeth posted to Krakow; Jewish Resistance crumbling

MARCH 1943: Gola Mira arrested

MARCH 13, 1943: Final aktzia of S.S.: Goeth invades "A" Ghetto with a force of S.S. men, Ukrainians, Latvians, Lithuanians, and Polish police. 9,000 Jews transferred to the Plaszow camp. The next day, Goeth invades "B" camp

FEBRUARY TO APRIL 1943: Gusta Davidson Draenger writes *Pamientnik Justyny*

MARCH 13, 1943: Jewish Fighting Organization bunker seized

APRIL 29, 1943: In separate break-outs, Szymek and Gusta Draenger escape from Montelupich Prison

JANUARY 1944: Forced labor camp at Plaszow becomes Kazetlager concentration camp

MAY 2, 1944: The liquidation of Plaszow, trucking out of children

Justyna's Narrative

Editors' Introduction

+>-<+

*Eli Pfefferkorn and
David H. Hirsch*

I<small>T HAD BEEN CUSTOMARY</small> for members of the Akiba Youth Movement in post–World War I Poland to assemble on Friday nights to celebrate the onset of the Sabbath. The festive table would be covered with a white cloth and adorned with Sabbath candles. Seated around the table, the young men and women welcomed the Sabbath with songs and poetry. By 1942, these gatherings took place inside the Krakow Ghetto, and the Akiba fighters were deeply engaged in life-threatening, anti-Nazi activities. On the Friday night of November 20, 1942, a movement leader expressed a premonition that this would be the last time they would greet the Sabbath together, and amidst the warm holiday spirit, someone uttered the words, "This is the Last Supper." The speaker was correct. Thereafter, that last evening in the Akiba meeting place at 13 Jozefinska Street was remembered as "The Last Supper."

It was Aharon Liebeskind, the spiritual leader of Akiba and at thirty its oldest member, who spoke that premonition. An ominous hush fell over those present, for they understood he was announcing the end of a long chapter in Jewish history. Soon after, the Akiba leadership decided to close down the Jozefinska apartment and move their operational activities outside the ghetto because of deteriorating conditions. This decision was the culmination of hours of agonized discussion among the youth, who were mounting challenges to both the German occupiers and the Jewish Council.

In making their choice, the young fighters faced some painful dilemmas: Where and when were they to mount their resistance to the enemy? If outside the ghetto, then in the city of Krakow or in the forests? Should they operate as Jewish units, or disperse and join up with the Polish resistance? Should they attack Jewish collaborators? Since they had no illusions that they were fighting to achieve a military victory, to what end should they pursue their struggle? Should their purpose be to avenge the wanton slaughter of nonbelligerent Jews, including children and elderly? To rescue themselves and their movement? To remain and fight to save Jewish honor?

The Krakow Ghetto had been sealed off on March 20, 1941, and by the time Aharon delivered his speech, the situation of the Jews in Poland was no longer tenable. Inside the Krakow Ghetto, it had become almost impossible for the underground to operate secretly. Despite the difficulties, however, the members of the Akiba Youth Movement—barely out of their teenage years—maintained their commune of kindred souls inside the ghetto. Drawing on each other for the strength to withstand the dehumanizing German occupation, they yearned for a past they knew was gone.

The spirit of communal life in that Jozefinska apartment was preserved in *Pamientnik Justyny,* which was written by Gusta Davidson Draenger while she was an inmate in the Montelupich Prison in Krakow. It records the deeds of the Krakow Jewish resistance in an epic style reminiscent of the great nineteenth-century Polish epic *Pan Tadeusz* by Adam Mickiewicz. Draenger's epic narrative of the resistance movement furnishes us with some understanding of the spirit that motivated the members of Akiba, whose "ideology combined most of the traditions and illusions of nineteenth-century European liberalism with a romantic belief in the ethical advantages of living in kibbutzim" (Ainsztein 1974, 830).

Driven by an acute historical consciousness and an instinct for collective survival, Draenger's intention was to erect a monument to a cohort of young Jewish men and women from a number of Jewish youth organizations who had buried ideological differences to confront a common enemy. But the spearhead of the resistance in Krakow were the members of the Akiba Youth Movement, headed by Aharon Liebeskind ("Dolek" in the *Narrative*); Gusta's husband, Shimshon (Szymek) Draenger ("Marek"); Gusta Davidson Draenger herself ("Justyna"); Abraham (Laban) Leibowicz ("Romek"); and Maniek Eisenstein.[1]

By the second half of 1942, the Germans were intent on genocide. Christopher Browning describes the situation succinctly: "In mid-March 1942, some 75 to 80 percent of all victims of the Holocaust were still alive, while 20 to 25 percent had perished. A mere eleven months later, in mid-February 1943, the percentages were exactly the reverse" (1993, xv). During the fall of 1942, Gusta and her husband, Szymek, found shelter in the Polish town of Rabka, outside of Krakow, by posing as Aryans. As head of the "technical department" of the Krakow Jewish resistance, Szymek forged identity cards and travel papers with Gusta's aid and maintained contact with resistance leaders in Krakow and its environs. In December 1942, the Jewish Fighting Organization of Krakow,[2] in collaboration with Jewish members of a Polish underground group, carried out its most effective series of raids against the Nazis. The raids were successful enough to merit a secret telegram from S.S. Grupenfuhrer Mueller of the Reichs-Security Main Office in Krakow to headquarters in Berlin that announced the shooting of Aharon Liebeskind and Juda Tenenbaum.[3]

---

1. It is not possible to enter into all of the intricacies of the coalitions between the youth groups that joined to form the Jewish Fighting Organization. But we must mention Heshek Bauminger of Hashomer Hatzair (a Marxist group), because he was among the most effective fighters.

2. According to Rivka Perlis, the Jewish Fighting Organization in Krakow (ZOB, or *Zydowska Organizacja Bojowa*) was composed of all of the Zionist youth movements, of which Akiba was the core. She states that the organization was founded in August 1942 (1984, 9). Yitzhak Zuckerman writes that the Jewish Fighting Organization was founded in Warsaw on July 28, 1942 (1993, 202). Shmuel Krakowski writes that it was "established . . . by the Zionist youth organization" (1993, 23).

3. The German text with an English translation is reprinted in Bauminger 1986, 77–79. The document was presented as evidence at the Eichmann trial. "Reichs-Security Main Office" is a literal translation of *Reichssicherheitshauptamt* (RSHA), a German organizational unit that brought together "the state security formations—the Secret State Police (Gestapo) and the Criminal Police (Kripo)—and the Nazi Party security service, the *Sicherheitsdienst* (SD). It was a

Gusta and Szymek had been a team since she was fifteen. Gusta had been introduced to the Akiba Youth Movement by a school chum, Rina Nezer, and it was through Akiba that Gusta Davidson met Szymek Draenger. Akiba opened to Gusta a world informed by idealism, self-sacrifice, and the goal of establishing a homeland in what was then Palestine. Though drawn to these ideals, Gusta was reluctant to break with the religious orthodoxy of her upbringing. The Akiba ideology combined the universalistic views of the Enlightenment with biblical humanistic values, replacing traditional messianic redemption theology with a Zionist ideology of redemption of the land by collective human effort. Joining Akiba meant adopting new values and breaking with her family. But she did so, and in recognition of her verbal talents, she was appointed to the editorial board of the newsletter *Young Pioneers*.

At the Akiba meetings, Szymek stood out as a natural leader. Those who knew him say he exhibited leadership qualities even as an adolescent. Szymek was stoic and not much given to expressing his emotions in sentimental language or gestures, while Gusta was highly expressive, gregarious, and eager to articulate her feelings. The two were instantly attracted to each other, and their friendship deepened into total devotion. Yet in a conversation with Eli Pfefferkorn at Kibbutz Degania in Israel in October 1987, Polish survivor Wushka Liebeskind (widow of fighter Aharon Liebeskind) recalled that Szymek was obsessively absorbed by his work in the underground. He demanded total obedience of his subordinates and was even more demanding of himself. "Sentiment, personal matters, even his relationship to Gusta—everything—all were replaced by the cause, which he regarded as sacred," she remembered.

Yehuda Maimon corroborates Wushka's observations, with one revealing exception. He had worked for Szymek, taking special assignments that made use of his Aryan appearance and unaccented Polish. In his Haifa apartment in October 1987, he relayed this story to Pfefferkorn:

---

central office both of the S.S. and of the Reich Interior Ministry" (Dear 1996, 969).

The love between Szymek and Gusta was unusual. He was rigid and not demonstrative, and you would sometimes think he was incapable of forming close relationships. But he loved Gusta dearly. Once Gusta was away on a mission to Kielce and was expected to return to the ghetto before curfew. Szymek assigned me to dress as a policeman and wait for her outside the ghetto. When she showed up, I was to escort her into the ghetto. I waited for hours, pacing back and forth, but she didn't show up. It was dangerous to hang out near the fence too long, and it was also getting very late. So I returned to the ghetto, only to receive a tongue-lashing from Szymek and orders to "get back to the rendezvous, and don't come back without Gusta." From a conspiratorial point of view, the order was out of line, and Szymek never would have given it if it hadn't been Gusta who was involved.

This commitment was mutual. When the Gestapo came to arrest Szymek for anti-Fascist activities in 1939, Gusta happened to be at his house. She instantly stepped forward. "I'm his fiancée," she is reported to have said, "and must go with him." They were both interned in the Troppau camp for six months and were released thanks to intervention on their behalf.[4]

The story of Gusta's imprisonment in January 1943 begins with the arrest of her husband as well. There are several versions of how Szymek came to be arrested, but the most authoritative witnesses are Yehuda Maimon, one of the youngest Akiba fighters, and Hela Rufeisen-Schipper, who smuggled weapons into the ghetto.[5] As Maimon told Pfefferkorn in October 1987, Szymek had helped plan

---

4. In his introduction to *Yomanah shel Yustina*, the Hebrew edition of *Pamientnik Justyny*, Nachman Blumental writes that Gusta and Szymek were taken to Troppau on October 22, 1939, and that they were released after their families paid a ransom to a Gestapo official (Draenger 1977, 116). See also Ainsztein 1974, 844.

5. Yehuda Maimon, who lives in Israel, is mentioned in the *Narrative* by his code name, Poldek. Hela Rufeisen-Schipper survived and lives in Israel. Her smuggling of the first weapons into the Krakow Ghetto from Warsaw is described in the *Narrative*. Hela was without doubt one of those heroic women singled out by Emmanuel Ringelblum when he says, "They are a great theme that calls for the pen of a great writer."

the December 1942 attacks against the S.S. and the Wehrmacht, and had then been ordered back to Rabka, where a courier was to inform him of the results of what came to be known as the Cyganeria operation.[6] After having waited a couple of days in vain for the courier to

---

6. The attacks of December 22, 1942, were the high point of the Krakow Jewish resistance. Several cafes and German hangouts were attacked, but the heaviest damage was inflicted in the Cyganeria Cafe. According to one estimate, "seven German officers [were] killed and many more wounded" (Bauminger 1986, 72). Hela Rufeisen-Schipper tells an interesting story about the aftermath of the attack in *Farewell to Mila 18* (1990, 89–90), translated here by Nessa Olshansky-Ashtar:

The next day, we left the hotel [in Warsaw]. I boarded yet another train, this time for Krakow; Samek headed in a different direction. I had virtually no money, and I realized that if I didn't run into a contact at the soup kitchen, I wouldn't know what to do next.

When we reached Krakow it was getting dark. There was just one other person in the car with me, a young academic from Krakow. During the trip, we had struck up a conversation, as travelers do, about such matters as the German occupation, the chances of the war's ending soon, the holiday season that had just ended, Poland's suffering. We had sighed in unison, and the pleasant young intellectual, trying to boost my spirits and encourage me to believe there was a brighter future ahead, whispered to me, "Listen, Madame, the war will soon be over."

"What makes you say that?"

"Madame, our forces have started to move. Take my word for it, they are already carrying out acts of sabotage, like blowing up railroad tracks, and I read in the underground paper that in Krakow, too, our boys, the Polish underground, have attacked German cafes with grenades and bombs, injuring and killing many Germans. How proud they make me!"

I couldn't control myself, I had to say something. Here I was a Jew, maybe the last one alive who knew the truth about who had carried out the attacks. The Warsaw Ghetto was being annihilated, most of the Krakow fighters were imprisoned, and it wasn't clear whether any of them would be able to escape the Germans' deadly clasp. Yet no one seemed to know that the deed had been part of the Jewish war against the Germans and had been carried out by Jewish fighters. This was one time, I decided, that I wouldn't be harming anyone other than myself if I spoke up — I had no addresses of contacts, no one to betray if I was interrogated.

"Listen, sir," I whispered. "You are an intelligent man, and, I would hope, a decent human being. I would like to let you in on a secret. I am returning from Warsaw, where a mass deportation is underway in the ghetto. And the Jews are fighting! They say that Warsaw will soon be *Judenrein,* free of Jews, that not one

report, Szymek went to Krakow to find out what had happened. He was recognized and turned in to the authorities.

In her book *Farewell to Mila 18* (Hebrew), Hela Rufeisen-Schipper adds detail to the tale. "Szymek," she writes, "had come up with the idea of forging Hungarian documents for Jewish-looking Jews, entitling them to live outside the ghetto. To produce them, he needed a genuine document to copy. He asked a Hungarian Jew named Saul to let him have his identity papers for a day; when the man refused, Szymek took them by force. Though Szymek returned them the same day, the Hungarian followed him and betrayed him to the Germans, who promptly seized him" (Rufeisen-Schipper 1990, 9; translated by Nessa Olshansky-Ashtar).

When Szymek failed to return to Rabka, where he and Gusta had been living, she went to Krakow to find him. While searching for Szymek in Krakow, she met Hela Schipper. Hela continues the tale:

> On January 17, I returned to Krakow, where I met Gusta Draenger on St. Philippa Street, not far from the train station. A young courier, Simek Lustgarten's brother Romek, was with her. She was distraught: her husband, Szymek, had left Rabka, where he had been living, a week ago, and there had been no word from him since. Although Szymek had to travel frequently, Gusta was always nervous when he was on the road. This time, all her inquiries into his whereabouts had proven fruitless. Now she had brought Witush, her five-year-old nephew and the son of her deported sister who had died, to stay with Hanka Blass, so that she could come into town herself to look for Szymek. But she had found no trace of him. I realized we couldn't leave her alone in such a state.

---

will remain alive. You ought to be aware, kind sir, that the attack to which you referred, on the Krakow cafes, was the work of young Jewish fighters. If you live to see the end of the war, please, tell the world about it. And by the way, I, too, am a Jew."

My words seemed to stun him. He was silent. We were approaching Krakow. As the train pulled into the station, he quietly asked me if I had somewhere to spend the night.

"Not really."

"I'll show you a place where people smuggling foodstuffs from the villages go." He led me to an apartment near the station. The atmosphere was far from pleasant, but no one there suspected me of being a Jew.

7

I tried to persuade her that Szymek had been planning to go to Warsaw and had discussed this plan with me. Had he gone to Warsaw, he may well have been unable to contact her. "Come to Warsaw with me, Gusta, we can look for him there," I suggested. We entered the soup kitchen run by the nuns. Julek was there. He too attempted to convince Gusta that Szymek might be in Warsaw. Not wanting to remain in one place too long but unable to continue our discussion in the street, for it was bitterly cold outside, we eventually rose and crossed over to the workers' cafeteria. Evening fell, and we had to decide what to do. We went over to the train station. At some point Gusta had expressed willingness to come to Warsaw with us, but she changed her mind at the last minute. "I can't go to Warsaw, it's too far away. I can't leave Witush . . . for so long. I have to get back to Rabka. You go look."

We parted. Gusta went off with Romek, and Samek (Julek) and I left for Warsaw. But Gusta didn't go back to Rabka. Despairing, she sensed that Szymek had been apprehended by the Germans; some preternatural intuition compelled her to keep searching for him. Whatever he was enduring, she wanted to be with him. Just as she had insisted on accompanying him to the Troppau camp at the beginning of the war, so she now made the rounds of all the German police stations in Krakow, seeking word of him. She went from station to station, asking whether her husband, Marek Borowski (his Polish underground pseudonym), was detained there. In the end she located the police station to which he had been taken, and, unable to bear parting from him, voluntarily joined her beloved husband.

Both she and Romek, who had been searching with her, were apprehended. They took Gusta to the Holtzlow Street Women's Prison; Romek was taken to a nearby jail, Montelupich, where Szymek had already been incarcerated. (Rufeisen-Schipper 1990, 86–87, translated by Nessa Olshansky-Ashtar)[7]

Eli Pfefferkorn asked why an idealist as dedicated to the cause as Gusta would commit so suicidal an act. Yehuda Maimon offered his opinion: "She was a fighter, she was a writer, she was an idealist, but

---

7. Szymek had been arrested by the Germans for his anti-Fascist publications in 1939, and Gusta had joined him then as well, in the Troppau concentration camp. This time, Gusta and Szymek escaped; Romek Lustgarten did not survive. Holtzlow Street Women's Prison was in the Montelupich Prison complex.

she was a woman first. Gusta had an unusually strong personality. In giving herself in to be with Szymek, she expressed her personality."

Soon after she was consigned to her cell, Gusta began composing and putting together the notes that were eventually published in Krakow as *Pamientnik Justyny*. These notes render in fairly close detail the smuggling of arms from Warsaw, the ambushing of Wehrmacht soldiers, the fate that befell the fighters in the forest, and other events apparently described by one who was a direct participant.

Since Gusta had spent most of her time in Rabka while those events occurred, one is led to wonder how she acquired so much firsthand information about the activities of the underground. Some of the information was, of course, derived from her own experiences on special missions. But she describes with an intense immediacy many events that she could neither have observed nor participated in. One source of information was Szymek, who determined operational policies in concert with Dolek and Laban. A second source was Gusta's fellow inmates, many of whom had served as liaisons between underground groups in different Polish cities.

In her prison cell in Montelupich, within the severe regimen of prison life, Gusta tapped her deep spiritual resources. To resist the incessant assaults on the humanity of the prisoners, Gusta organized a daily routine that revolved around discussions of philosophy, history, literature, the Bible, and an array of other subjects. Gusta and those imprisoned with her spent much of their time reciting poetry and composing new poems, some of which the survivors still remember. After a group of inmates had been taken out to be shot, those left behind would give vent to their sadness in song. They were resigned to death, but resolved not to give in to despair.

Another extraordinary occupant of that cell was Gola Mira, who in Gusta's narrative is credited with setting up the links between the Krakow Jewish resistance and the Polish Workers' Party. Gola was a fervent idealist, and like Gusta was a woman of a literary bent. In a conversation with Eli Pfefferkorn, survivor Genia Meltzer attests:

Gola spent her time writing poetry in Yiddish. She also recited poetry. For me this was a new experience. My family didn't speak Yiddish. I understood the language, but I couldn't speak it. And I knew nothing about Yiddish poetry. Once I was so moved by Gola's reading that I went over to her and said, "Gola, I never knew Yiddish before. You opened a whole new world to me and it is such a moving world. But now I am sorry, so sorry that I will never be able to enter that world because this is the end. What I have learned here from you is all that I will ever learn."

Although Gusta was a Zionist and Gola a Communist, the two were very close. Such a difference didn't matter in Cell 15. Gola was admired by all of us. They used to come in and take her away for interrogation at their headquarters at Pemorska, and when they brought her back, she had bruises all over her body. They beat her mercilessly. They shaved her head, and every part of her body was black and blue. She was in this state the first time I saw her, when I came into the cell, and it was in this state that she composed her Yiddish songs and poetry.

Even as she was shaping the contours of prison life, Gusta was deploying her intellectual energies to figure out a way to write the story of the underground. Careful planning was required to overcome what appeared to be insurmountable obstacles. The success of the endeavor depended on maintaining complete secrecy in a hostile environment. Apart from the prison wardens, who used to barge into the cell unexpectedly, some of her cell-mates had been arrested for prostitution, smuggling, and other illegal activities, and were not known to be entirely trustworthy.

In the relatively spacious cell (seven by seven meters, housing about fifty people), Gusta claimed a private corner next to the barbed-wire window. A handful of women huddled together in a circle, and in the center of the circle sat Gusta, inscribing tiny letters on scraps of paper. When her fingers became numb from exertion, another woman would take over the writing while Gusta dictated. Every single note was checked by Gusta before being stashed away. In a 1989 interview with Eli Pfefferkorn, Elsa Lapa remembers how the women would urge Gusta to get on with the writing while she was verifying the facts. "We haven't got much time left, Gusta. Any moment they may come and take us away," they would tell her. But Gusta would not budge. "This is history, and it must be accurate," she insisted.

Gusta began writing the notes on toilet paper given out to the inmates. When this supply ran out, she turned for paper and pencils to a group of Jewish auto mechanics who worked for the Gestapo during the day and were housed in the Montelupich Prison at night.

The nature of their work allowed them some leeway to move around in the prison courtyard, and from there they established contact with the women by facial gestures and hand signals. Edek Friedman and Romek Morovitz tell about the ingeniously contrived channels through which they smuggled in writing materials and smuggled out the first batches of notes. Edek tried to read the notes by the dim light of the prison cell, but the letters were too tiny to make out. Two complete sets of notes were hidden in the prison, and another two were smuggled out. Only one set survived; it is deposited in the museum of Kibbutz Lohamei Haghetaot (the Ghetto Fighters Kibbutz) in Israel.

What motivated Gusta to undertake the dangerous and seemingly impossible task of writing the history of the resistance, even under the vigilant eyes of the prison wardens? Like Emmanuel Ringelblum in Warsaw and Isaac Rudashevski in Vilna, to mention only two, Gusta was driven by the threat of oblivion — the fear that the memory of the Jewish people would vanish. Gusta wished to preserve not only that memory, but also the spirit of defiance the Jewish underground fighters cultivated against the Nazi death machine. She states her purpose in the very first lines of her notes, which are in the museum archives, but not in the published Polish book: "From this prison cell that we will never leave alive, we young fighters who are about to die salute you. We offer our lives willingly for our holy cause, asking only that our deeds be inscribed in the book of eternal memory. May the memories preserved on these scattered bits of paper be gathered together to compose a picture of our unwavering resolve in the face of death."

Elsa Lapa described the painstaking writing process itself to Eli Pfefferkorn. Her account is worth reproducing in full.

> I remember as if it were today. The images live in my memory: Gusta sitting in the middle, surrounded by the girls to conceal the fact that she was writing, in case one of the guards should look through the peep hole or suddenly sneak up on us. Peshka and I are sitting near the barred window, on the lookout for the boys who work in the garage to get information from them.[8] Gusta was wor-

---

8. Peshka is Pesia Warszawski. She was one of the fighters in Heshek Bauminger's group.

ried that she wouldn't have time enough to finish writing the story, that she would be taken out before she could finish the tale. "Who will write our story?" she kept on asking. She was frantic. Day and night she wrote, or when not writing, dictated to the girls. And she was meticulous. She would check every word, every sentence. She worked at writing the *Pamientnik* from January to March 13 [1943].

I can tell you why the writing sometimes seems fragmentary. When they brought me into the cell, Gusta stopped writing and started to question me about my activities, about my friends, where I had been. This was true of every new entrant into the cell. Gusta is surrounded by the girls as she writes. Suddenly the prison door opens and two sisters are admitted: Hanka and Luska Spritzer. Immediately, Gusta stops writing and starts questioning the girls. Another day, Genia Meltzer is shoved into the cell. She was not part of the underground, but we knew her from the Gymnazium. She was caught on Aryan papers. Gusta questions her, making mental notes.

We wrote four copies. We hid one copy inside the stove that was placed in the cell. Gusta said that the stove would never be lit, anyway. Another we hid inside the upholstery covering the door; a third we passed through a window for either the boys working in the garage or a member of the Polish underground to pick up; and the fourth we hid under the floor. I have the feeling that we wrote much more, and that some was lost. All of it is written on toilet paper that we used to get from the prison warden. The pencils were given to us by Polish girls, who used to receive food parcels from home with hidden pieces of pencils in them.[9]

Gusta had a natural flair for writing. She would finish writing a page and then read it out to us, which would be followed by copying. She was afraid that some of the writing might be discovered, and that's why she wrote only about events already known to the Gestapo. She also encoded the names for the same reason. She desperately hoped that somehow one copy would reach our members in Kibbutz Kfar Yehoshuah, in the *Yishuv* [Jewish community in Palestine]. All these things seem very trivial now. But for us at the time every step we took had vital significance.

---

9. The varied claims regarding sources of writing materials are all likely to be correct; Gusta and her cohorts gathered tools from every available source.

When not writing, we participated in seminars, discussing what the world would look like after the war, believing that this would be the last war; we studied Hebrew and challenged our minds. Gusta tried to arrange everything in a collective manner. We ate our daily portion of bread, 110 grams each, together; we kept up the tradition of Oneg Shabbat with singing and poetry recitation.

Another former inmate of that cell who lives now in Israel, Genia Meltzer, described Gusta's spiritual influence to Pfefferkorn.[10] She described as well the significance that the *Pamientnik* itself began to acquire for the imprisoned women. When first thrown into the cell, Genia attests,

> I couldn't eat. I couldn't drink. I couldn't communicate at all with the others. I just sat alone in the corner of the cell, trying to regain my bearings. I sat there, just thinking. I was trying to reach down into myself, to discover some hidden strength that would enable me to go on. I was trying to recover from the shock. The natural tendency was to surrender yourself to the place, to give up your humanity. But Gusta's leadership prevented us from succumbing. Now I will tell you something surprising: that place, known only for torture and death, actually became a place of life to me. It had a life's rhythm. And that rhythm emanated from Gusta Draenger.
>
> Although she firmly believed that we could expect nothing but an early and violent death, she didn't let us neglect ourselves. She made us wash and brush our hair every day, as long as the water lasted. A basin of water was brought in to us daily. And she made certain that the table was cleaned every day. We used to have roll calls twice a day. She saw to it that we kept ourselves and our cell clean. She believed that by doing these things, by cleaning and being orderly, we would keep our spirits up and retain our humanity. She never believed that we would survive the place. But she felt that while we were alive, we should behave as human beings.
>
> Of course Gusta's time went into writing and dictating *Pamientnik Justyny*, her memoir of the movement. Several of us took part in copying the diary. You can find many different handwritings. When Gusta was tired, her hands grew too weak to write, so she dictated to one of us. Then we copied from one set to another.

---

10. Genia Meltzer's story is also told in Zuckerman and Bassok, n.d., 323.

The *Pamientnik* was written on triangular pieces of toilet paper, which we sewed together using threads unraveled from our skirts and a needle. We kept the writings hidden in a hole we had found in the padded covering of the cell door.

In the situation we were in — knowing that each day might be our last — a human being looks for meaning, for purpose, for beauty. Of course there were some who simply sat in the corner, filled with fear. But we searched for meaning. As I lay there each night, I thought: This is the end. This is the end. And I too was overcome by fear. But we did have a source of meaning in our lives. Although we knew that we would die, we also knew that the diary would survive us. This knowledge saved us from despair. All we cared about was for the diary to survive.

The time frame of *Justyna's Narrative* is relatively brief, and divides roughly into four stages. The historical events occur in a span of about four months.[11] The deceptively peaceful Kopaliny episode marks the first critical stage of the struggle, when the leaders realize they must give up their pacifist ideals as well as their hope of transforming the masses by educating them in the enchantments of "high" culture and egalitarian principles. The second stage, which begins with Gusta's entry into "the quarter" (the Krakow Ghetto), marks the leaders' painfully frustrating attempts, accompanied by innumerable setbacks, to shift from a cultural to a conspiratorial organization. Draenger conveys the stagnation the fighters felt in trying to get the conspiracy going. Starting with almost no military training, little knowledge of conspiratorial activity, and no outside help, they had to go through an arduous process of trial and error.

In the third stage of the narrative, Gusta depicts the actual armed struggle. Again, the fighters experience more frustration than success, and Gusta does not try to mask the operational failures. If anything, she gives them more space than the successes. Nor does

---

11. The Kopaliny farm episode takes place sometime in August 1942; Gusta's entry into the ghetto seems to have happened in early September. The first group of five was sent into the forest on September 20. "The Last Supper" was held on November 20, and the headquarters at 13 Jozefinska was abandoned on November 25, 1942.

she minimize the quixotic element in their enterprise, as when she describes the arrival of the first weapons: "Marek is busy breaking down the Browning. He is as happy as a child just given the toy he's always dreamed of. It's hard to tell who is happier, the man who has finally gotten his hands on an implement of destruction or the boy who has found a plaything."

The final phase is the collapse of the movement. Here the narrative becomes somewhat obscure. The last ten pages or so portray the accelerating slide into confusion and ruin. Detailed accounts are given of the capture of Wushka Liebeskind, the capture and escape of her husband, Aharon (Dolek), and the police's pursuit of Laban Leibowicz (Romek). The leaders of the movement are being hunted down and taken into captivity or killed. The ghetto headquarters at 13 Jozefinska will soon be abandoned, and the fighters are about to be dispersed. The bucolic ripeness and summer glow of Kopaliny have withered into a ghetto scene of winter and impending doom: "As the first rays of daybreak stole through the windowpanes, they slowly began to rise from their beds. A new day had arrived — a gloomy, dreary day." So ends the *Narrative* proper.

In Draenger's telling, the duly recorded tactical setbacks are redeemed by a counterpoint of moral and spiritual triumph. It is easy to miss the artistry with which she creates this counterpoint, because she appears to be following a simple chronology of events. But by telescoping some events and expanding others, and by alternating prose narrative with poetic description, she strikes a note of joy that overwhelms the despair. The two middle stages of the narrative — the getting started and the guerrilla attacks — are structurally balanced by the poetically rendered tranquility of Kopaliny at the start and the magnificent description of "The Last Supper," which momentarily interrupts the accelerating disintegration of the movement just before the end of the *Narrative*. The mood generated by these two scenes counteracts the despair and frustration occasioned by the declining fortunes of the Jewish resistance fighters.

How does Draenger create a sense of redemptive glory that outweighs the operational setbacks? An entry in *Scroll of Agony: The Warsaw Diary of Chaim A. Kaplan*, one of the most moving ghetto diaries — which embodies not only the lucid commentaries of a highly attentive observer, but also the reflections of a learned and profound thinker — provides the beginnings of an answer. On January 4, 1942, after nearly two and a half years of German occupation and a year before Draenger was taken into captivity and began her narrative, Kaplan writes:

> The words of the poet have come true in all their dreadful meaning: " 'Tis not a nation nor a sect but a herd." Gone is the spirit of Jewish brotherhood. The words "compassionate, modest, charitable" no longer apply to us. The ghetto beggars who stretch out their hands to us with the plea, "Jewish hearts, have pity!" realize that the once tender hearts have become like rocks. Our tragedy is the senselessness of it all. Our suffering is inflicted on us because we are Jews, while the real meaning of Jewishness has disappeared from our lives. (Kaplan 1973, 289)

Kaplan recognizes that the devastating results of ghettoization (starvation, disease, the constant threat of inexplicable punishment or deportation, the ubiquitous terror, and the gradual dehumanization of the ghetto populace) have taken their toll. Ironically, as Kaplan observes, the people being persecuted because they are Jews have been robbed of some key tenets of their Jewishness: compassion, modesty, communal spirit. It is these values that Draenger maintains in her narrative.

Unlike most ghetto diaries, *Justyna's Narrative* does not dwell on the day-to-day squalor, deprivation, and sadism of ghetto life. Whatever the hardships and cruelties of the Krakow Ghetto, it is not Draenger's purpose to portray them. On the contrary, her purpose is to reveal a small group of people who have made a deliberate decision not to yield to the machinery of dehumanization. Draenger captures the aura of exaltation arising out of the solidarity of the Akiba youth group. The rarefied atmosphere of their communal existence can be felt in her description of the farm at Kopaliny, and this atmosphere is sustained throughout. When she describes her entrance into the quarter in Krakow, for example, she emphasizes the euphoria she feels from being back among her comrades after completing the risky mission of securing her parents and in-laws outside the ghetto.

Following the October 1942 deportations, the fighters undergo a transition forced upon them by circumstances, a shift from allegiance to the traditional nuclear and extended Jewish family to total loyalty to the family of resistance fighters. The deportations have left many movement youths bereft of family obligations. These youths can now commit themselves to their goal and to each other, and experience the gift of life with renewed fervor. They will not permit their lives to be drained away by their enemy's malice.

The narrative culminates in the final "Greeting the Sabbath" meal at 13 Jozefinska. The leaders know they will soon have to abandon their temporary haven. The endgame is about to start, and Dolek is keenly aware of what is coming. If Gusta's capitulation of his statement to the members of Akiba were translated "literally," it would sound like a speech out of *Beowulf*. In Draenger's writing, matter-of-fact descriptions in a more colloquial Polish mingle with poetic metaphors and a heroic epic style; observations on everyday life in the ghettoes are set beside dramatic dialogue and philosophical reflection. It must be remembered that Draenger wrote under tremendous pressure and in severely constrained conditions. She did not have time for leisurely reflection and certainly could not afford the luxury of extensive revision. Because she was writing in a prison cell about an ongoing conspiracy against the Nazis, Draenger had to disguise the actual names of the historical characters and to remain vague about place and chronology. Hence it is sometimes difficult to follow the comings and goings to and from the ghetto. It is also quite possible that in her prison cell Gusta was not able to keep track of time, so some of the vagueness may simply reflect her inability to place events precisely. But she was as interested in the inner truth of events as in chronological exactitude.

Readers may wonder what happened to the author and her husband. While it is not precisely clear how they died, it was not in the Montelupich Prison, from which they both escaped on the same day, April 29, 1943, though in unconnected breaks. In her October 1987 interview with Eli Pfefferkorn, Genia Meltzer tells how the women escaped.

> We knew that in the next transport they would take the rest of us, and it occurred to Gusta and me simultaneously that we should try to make a break. When our turn came to be taken out for transport, we would not go along with the S.S. plan, but would shape our deaths in our own way. Gola, Gusta, and I got together and started

planning. Peshka also participated. Because we used to watch the other transports, we knew exactly what they would do with us. They would take us out, then bring us across to the Montelupich Yard, and then to Plaszow.

We realized our escape would not be of great significance. It was no big deal. We just wanted to show there were female Jewish prisoners who had disrupted the S.S. plan, who had refused to follow their script. On the evening prior to our transport, they came in for the final roll call. Gusta stood in front as usual and reported the number present to the guard. After the counting, he left. Usually after the evening roll call, we would take the mattresses down, spread them out on the floor, and go to sleep or talk, but this evening we did not take the mattresses down. Instead, we huddled together and sang Hatikva. We knew that the next morning we would be taken to death.

You would probably expect us to prepare for death separately, to take stock of ourselves individually. But we didn't. We stayed together. The following morning, the jailer came in with the list. She started calling out names and ordered us to take our bundles with us. They took us out into the corridor. There were twenty-five to thirty of us, and two jailers. One of the jailers unlocked the door, and we went down the stairs to the yard outside. As we began crossing the yard, we suddenly heard sounds of life. Cars. People walking. Life. But we were walking to our deaths. As if nothing were happening, the world outside sounded the same. But we were going to die.

They took us to the gate, the Ukrainian guard opened it, and we went through. In front of us stood a German, to our left a jailer, on the other side, another German. The one leading us held the list. All of them were armed, of course. We walked toward the lane where the main section of Montelupich is located. We first reached the pavement, then the sidewalk. At this point, Wushka was supposed to yell, "*Viatch!*" Scatter! She did say "Viatch," but she didn't say it loud enough.

The German leading us was already on the other side of the street. He turned to us, expectantly. We were supposed to walk toward him and get onto the truck. But we stopped instead. He held the list and just stared at us. He noticed something was wrong. Something unusual was happening. Then he smiled and said, "Come on over here." But still, we didn't move forward. His face filled with astonishment: What is happening? We could see fear in his eyes. Something was going to happen that he could not predict, and he was afraid.

The German who was standing on our right blocked our way to the main street. He was standing near me. When I saw him raise his arm and point his gun, I ran around behind him, then slipped under his outstretched arms, pushing it up into the air with my head. The gun went up, giving us a second to start running.

We ran into the street. Just then a horse and buggy drove by. We ran around it and kept going. They were shooting at us constantly. But the horse and buggy blocked their view. People were falling here and there. We ran and ran. I was running with Sima. We saw the stairway of a train station and ran up. There was a building. We stopped at the door of an apartment and knocked. A woman came to the door, holding a baby in her arms. "Please hide us. The Germans are shooting. Please! Please! Hide us! They're shooting!"

"I can't," she answered, and I said, "Let's go. Sima. We don't want to endanger the baby. We'll find another place."

Sima and I went through the gate of a nearby house. There we found Gola. She was bleeding. We asked her to come with us, but she refused. She was afraid she'd put us in danger, so she ran away from us.

Then we went into a courtyard. There was a fence with a huge iron door. Between the door and the fence was a narrow opening that looked like a good place to hide. "Sima, Sima, come on, let's hide in there," I said, but Sima said, "It's no good." Then I heard a shot. But I was already in the hiding place.

I lay down. I stayed there. Many, many shots were fired all around me. Germans were running all around yelling: "Did you see Jews running here? Did you see a blond Jewess running this way? A blond Jewess?"

They answered that a blond Jewess had been there and had run away. So the Germans left the courtyard. They never looked behind the door. It became quiet. I lay very still.

I asked myself, "What? Am I still alive?" Then I heard the Poles talking among themselves. They were saying that Jews had escaped from prison and many of them had been killed. Shortly they left and went into their homes.[12]

---

12. Genia's story is also printed in Zuckerman and Bassok, n.d., 323.

Genia Meltzer survived to tell her story, but the last chapter of Gusta and Szymek's lives is shrouded in mystery. It is known that after their escape from prison they reunited in the town of Bochnia, near Krakow, where there was a strong Akiba contingent. They continued to resist the Germans in the forests around the Krakow area, and resumed publication of the underground newspaper *Hechalutz Halochem* (The fighting pioneer)[13] to fan the flames of resistance. Articles in the newspaper urge Poles to refuse to cooperate with the criminal regime, and try to persuade Jews not to submit meekly to the authorities. It is not always clear who wrote what, but it is a fair guess that Szymek wrote the political and ideological pieces, and that the more poetic articles that probed human psychology and motivation were written by Gusta.

There is a striking essay in Number 33 of *Hechalutz Halochem*, dated September 20, 1943, that analyzes the behavior of the guards in the Montelupich Prison. The piece is thought-provoking, and it may contain the last words Gusta ever wrote. It is entitled "Montelupich from the Viewpoint of Survivors":

At the top of the pecking order in Montelupich are the S.D., who rarely come in contact with the prisoners; directly beneath them are the S.S., who do the bidding of the S.D.; below them are the Ukrainian guards, master torturers. The *Schupo*, who occupy the lowest rung, are the ones most often in contact with the prisoners. They are more likely than the others to show mercy and even compassion. But in the presence of their superiors, they become hangmen, the cruelest of prison guards.

Tribal and nationalistic hatred and racial animosity are an ideological superstructure that masks a human predilection for cruelty and sadism. Though racial hatred may increase their animalism, its absence doesn't totally eliminate the bestiality of the jailers. It's not the German or the Ukrainian who tortures the Jew or the Pole. It is the beast lodged in human form that wields the levers of power inflicting pain on us.

And yet not all of them are the same. Not in all has savagery taken root so deep that they cannot occasionally suspend it. There

---

13. Though the newspaper's title was in Hebrew, the articles were written in Polish.

are S.D. people who, in spite of their ideological anti-Semitism or hatred of Poles, are unable to torture or inflict pain. At times, an S.S. soldier may come your way whose voice betrays genuine regret at the sight of a bludgeoned prisoner returning from an interrogation. And one can only hope that beneath the uniform and the death's-head symbol lives a soul free of sadism who is behaving in contradiction to the laws of nature.

Sometimes you come across a nineteen-year-old Ukrainian boy, still shaping dreams that hatched in the wide wheat fields of his homeland. He was compelled to come here by the war, and soon his dreams will be washed away in the sea of Montelupich barbarity.

In her last published words, we see Draenger struggling to retain her idealistic image of the human form, but requiring herself at the same time to acknowledge a new reality imposed by her experience of Nazi brutality. Her still-glowing hopes have been tempered. She vacillates between attributing the conditions of Montelupich to an evil inherent in the human form or to a system that brings out the worst. Draenger refers to the Ukrainian guards as master torturers, but then ponders the case of a Ukrainian boy who might have lived a decent life, had he just been left to realize "dreams that hatched in the wide wheat fields of his homeland."

The best available information indicates that Gusta's voice of hope was silenced forever in a skirmish with the Germans in the Wisnicz forest.[14]

---

14. This information was conveyed to Eli Pfefferkorn in interviews with survivors. Ainsztein writes as follows: "Only the death of Wodzislawski in October and the capture first of Gusta and finally of her husband, which occurred on 8 November 1943, put an end to the activities of the Jewish fighting Organization in Cracow" (1974, 849).

Introduction to the
Polish Edition, 1945

On December 12, 1941, a delegation of the Jewish Self-Help Society in Nowy Wisnicz (eight kilometers from Bochnia) sent a letter to the chief of the Gestapo, which contained among other things a request for "approval of a series of courses to be offered for the purpose of retraining the Jewish youth to do farm work, [and] . . . permission to establish a farm in Kopaliny."

Neither the chief of the Gestapo nor the *Landkommision* in Bochnia realized that by approving the society's request they were contributing to the efforts of a Jewish fighting group that planned to use the agricultural program to train resistance fighters.

Shimshon Draenger (known to everyone as Szymek), his wife, Gusta, Julius Feldhorn, and I were all approved for positions on the farm, with Szymek designated the person in charge.

In April or May of 1942, the new educational director of the Presidium, Adolf (Dolek) Liebeskind, arrived in Nowy Wisnicz. Dolek belonged to the inner circle of the Jewish Self-Help Society's presidium in the old General Government, but except for Dr. Hilfstein, none of the members knew that Dolek's reason for taking over as educational director was to keep in touch more easily with the various youth groups. As a representative of the presidium, he attended meetings of the Judenrat and other official committees during the day, but on his first night in Nowy Wisnicz he also participated in the initial resistance meeting, which was conducted behind locked doors and shuttered windows. The presidium members did not know that letters being mailed through the official auspices of the Jewish Self-Help Society contained the first instructions issued by the Jewish Fighting Organization in Krakow.

At that first secret meeting in Nowy Wisnicz, we read bulletins sent from Warsaw carrying news of a sealed railroad car filled with gas in Chelmno, and of other murderous acts committed by the Germans against the Jews in the captured eastern territories. It was decided that if we were to resist the Germans effectively, we would have to consolidate the youth groups. After Dolek left, the "seminars" he had organized continued to meet. We would debate about Hitlerism and Hitler's threats to exterminate the Jews while neutral books on such subjects as botany, zoology, and chemistry lay on the table unopened. Boys and girls listened to the lecturers with pride, though for security purposes the number of course participants was limited.

After six weeks, ten of the most trusted students were assigned to Kopaliny. These students were well schooled in theory and deemed ready to undertake practical work. During the day they did, in fact, work as farm trainees, but at night they mailed out bulletins, for our mission at that time was to disseminate accurate information.

From time to time Szymek and I travelled to Krakow to report to the presidium of the Jewish Self-Help Society, demand aid and supplies, and confer with Dolek on questions of how to organize and coordinate a meaningful Jewish resistance movement.

To outsiders our activities appeared innocent; nevertheless, the Jews in Nowy Wisnicz started to whisper that something must be cooking in Kopaliny. Finally, the Judenrat, most of whom had sold out to the enemy, warned us that we would have to close down the farm. We had the support of the Jewish Presidium Committee of the Self-Help, however, who defended us as their own coworkers and pointed out that we had been given a stamp of approval and official sanction by the chief of the Gestapo.

But we ourselves were not certain how to proceed. We were constantly debating ways and means, short-range versus ultimate goals, and were always dickering about what we could and could not hope to achieve.

-+->-<+-

Up to now, each one of us had been engrossed in his own affairs and in looking after his own interests. None of us had received any schooling in arms or in organizing; nor did any of us have military experience. We did not have much confidence in our own strength, and at first we did not even consider it possible to link up with any of the Polish fighting organizations already in existence.

It was at about that time that Dolek and Szymek met Gola Mira, a Communist, who was helpful in setting up contacts with P.P.R., a Polish underground movement.

To give some sense of the atmosphere of those initial meetings and of the discussions that took place at them, it is first necessary to describe the leaders of the Jewish Fighting Organization.

Dolek (Adolf Liebeskind, alias Jan Ropa, also known as Aharon), a law student and an intellectual, was the general secretary of the Zionist youth group Akiba. Decisive and unrelenting, he was prepared to sacrifice not only himself but those he held dearest, and he demanded no less from those around him. He was the first to volunteer for every fighting action, even though he knew that Szymek was much better suited for such work.

Szymek (Shimson Draenger, alias Marek Borowski) was a humanist with a degree in liberal arts; he edited *Divrei Akiba* (The sayings of Akiba). A tough, bellicose character, he despised all sorts of sentimentality. His chief aide was his wife, Gusta ("Justyna" in the narrative), who was also an active member of Akiba. Both were interned in the Troppau concentration camp during the first year of the war.

Laban (Abraham Leibowicz, "Romek" in the narrative) was an active member of the Zionist-Socialist organization Dror-Freiheit; he was a man of great courage whose youthful enthusiasm was contagious.

The youngest member of the Akiba group was Maniek Eisenstein.

As soon as the occupation began, these young people who were to become leaders of the Jewish resistance started thinking about the possibility of obtaining weapons and going into the forest, since many stories and rumors were already being circulated about groups of partisans. When the practical work started, the leadership was centered in the Krakow Ghetto. Dolek took it upon himself to procure weapons, provide military training, and send groups out into the forest. Szymek's task was to organize the technical bureau, and Laban took on the responsibility of raising money for the organization.

→>-<+

It is not easy to describe all the obstacles that had to be overcome in order to organize a Jewish resistance under Nazi occupation. Our work was a hundred times more difficult than the work of any other resistance group, because we had to conceal not only our underground activity but also, and even more urgently, our Jewish identities.

Hence it may be said that the first thing the leaders had to do was to deny even to themselves the impossibility of the task before them, and to act in spite of the overwhelmingly unfavorable odds. After convincing themselves that resistance was a realistic option, their next task was to break through the apathy and passivity of the Jewish masses.

→>-<+

The first group sent out to the forest by Dolek consisted of six young boys: Samuel Gottlieb, Baruch Weksner, Edwin Weiss, Salo Kanal, Zygmunt Mahler, and Fishel (I can't remember his last name). Their history is brief. Shortly after their arrival in the forest, somebody from the village reported to the German gendarmes that there were three hundred partisans operating in the area. The Germans surrounded the forest and shot at random; after a while they left. The next night our boys attacked the police station. Thinking they were being attacked by a large group, the police barricaded themselves so that our small group could not get them. A few days later, the gendarmes found our guys in a house not far from the forest. Again, somebody had informed on them. Three armed Germans came in. A shoot-out ensued in which two Germans were hit, but in the final analysis the first experiment was a dismal failure. Only one of the six Jewish fighters (Zygmunt Mahler) managed to get out alive. The main reason for the failure was the lack of weapons. The entire group had only two guns, and their plan had been to use those guns to come up with additional weapons.

This first abortive action hardened the resistance movement's resolve to acquire more weapons. The leaders also decided to concentrate our activities in the city for the time being, because of the fall weather and the difficulty of operating in the forest without the cooperation of the indigenous population.

Szymek lived in Myslenicy at that time, where he established a technical bureau that he later moved to Rabka. By forging train tickets, passes allowing entry into the ghetto, foreign papers, Aryan documents (*Kennkarte*), and so on, he made it possible for members of the Jewish resistance to move about with relative ease. The forgeries were so well done that officials could not believe the signatures on the false documents were not their own.

Juda Tennenbaum supplied the original blanks, which he stole from the office of the Gestapo, and Szymek used all of his drawing and technical skills to make those perfect forgeries.

The technical bureau brought in a large income, which eased Laban's job of fundraising. Nobody knew where Laban got the money. He would always come into the room with a wise smile, as if from another planet, and lay the foreign currency, Polish money, and gold on the table. He would not say anything. He would just smile.

→>─<─

Operating in Krakow, the seat of the occupying power, the Jewish resistance killed its first German in the park between Starowlisna Street and Serego Street. Dolek did the job.

He also took part in the later actions. Germans were now being killed by Jews on the streets of Krakow. One of the targets was a German flyer. The fighters also succeeded in sabotaging the tracks at the station in Krakow-Bochnia.

Subsequently, the Jewish fighting force in the ghetto contacted the P.P.R., whose head was Henri Bauminger. Operating in concert, the Jewish fighting force and the P.P.R. carried out an attack that shook the German authorities.

On the evening of December 22, 1942, Jewish fighters threw grenades into the Cyganeria coffee shop. Tens of Germans were hit, and several died of the wounds inflicted by Jewish girls and boys. The organization put up anti-German flyers and hung out red and white flags. The activities of the Jewish resistance were now forcing the Germans to take notice; the curfew hour was moved to six o'clock, and the occupation authorities took more severe repressive measures. Despite Gestapo vigilance, however, the attacks continued. Grenades were lobbed onto the main station in Krakow, and several coffeehouses frequented by the *Whermacht* in Kielce were bombed, as well as a movie house in Radom.

The Gestapo now stepped up their efforts and managed to trap a group of fighters hiding out in the ruins of the hospital on Stawinska Street. One of those hiding there was Laban. That whole group was captured by the Germans. Thanks to informers, the Gestapo also caught Alexander Goldberg (Alek), who lived in the contact apartment, at Wielopole 26.

On December 24, 1942, unaware of what had happened, Juda Tennenbaum came to the Jewish hospital on Dolek's instructions and was also taken by the Gestapo. The Gestapo found Adolf Liebeskind's address on Juda's Polish kennkarte, which enabled them to track Dolek down and execute him. He had lived like a hero and he died a hero. When the Gestapo came to Lutawskiego Street to pick him up, he killed two Germans and wounded two more before being taken down by a German bullet. . . .

On April 29, 1943, some of the prisoners in the Montelupich Prison were shot. Shimshon and Gusta managed to escape on the same day, though in separate actions, while Laban's attempt to get away failed. When he was trapped in the Jewish cemetery at Jerusalem Street, the site of mass executions of Jews, he attacked the S.S. man pursuing him and defended himself with his bare hands. He died after having been shot nine times.

Szymek (from then on Victor) returned to the area of Bochnia, where he rejoined Justyna, who had escaped from prison at the same time. Along with Hillel Wodzislawski, they organized a new Jewish fighting group in the Bochnia area, where they put out a small conspiratorial newspaper, *Hechalutz Halochem* (The fighting pioneer).

In November 1943, Szymek and Gusta disappeared. How they died is not known. Only one thing is certain: they were caught by the Germans. That is how the Jewish fighting force in Krakow was liquidated.

→>-<-

The memoir offered here to the reading public was written by Szymek Draenger's wife, Gusta, whose maiden name was Davidson. She wrote the diary in the Krakow prison on Helclow Street, between January and April of 1943, at which time she was twenty-five years of age.

Gusta was an attractive, intelligent woman of great charm. Her love for Szymek transformed her in some significant ways. As a young man, Szymek was a rather dry, humorless person. He had lived a hard life and always conducted himself in conformity to a set of high ideals. He was fiercely independent, possessed a strong fighting spirit, and placed abstract principles above personal ambitions.

Gusta was a completely dedicated woman with a deep soul and a warm, generous heart. Her husband's rigidity and his rigorous adherence to high ideals seemed to cast a shadow on Gusta's bright, playful disposition. But when the Jewish fighting force was formed in Krakow, Gusta-Justyna became the soul of the conspiratorial undertaking, and not one of the fighting deeds successfully undertaken could have been accomplished without her inspiration and work.

She did the technical work, sought out hiding places for the inexperienced revolutionaries, accompanied the first fighting groups to the forest, took part in numerous consultations among the leaders, brought guns, and suffered in silence because her husband, Szymek, did not have time for her. She suffered but she understood what was driving him, and she encouraged him to keep on fighting. After Szymek was arrested in 1943, I received a letter from Gusta-Justyna that ended with these words: "I would like to write the epic of my life and death, which will come soon."

That letter disturbed me, so I immediately dispatched a messenger to bring her to me in Bochnia. But Justyna had other plans. The next day the messenger returned with the news that Szymek's wife had gone to the police and given herself up of her own free will.

She wanted to see her husband one more time.

→>-<←

Some time later, I wound up in the Montelupich Prison in Krakow with Szymek. He told me that during the hearings they confronted him with Gusta in front of the chief of the Gestapo, who wanted to get a confession out of him — pointing to her wounds and to the bruises on her body. But Gusta-Justyna remained defiant, proclaiming proudly, "Yes, we organized Jewish fighting groups, and we promise you that if we succeed in getting out of your hands, we will organize a much stronger group of partisans."

I remember those words very well, and I understood at the time that with her words and her defiance, Gusta-Justyna was trying to reconcile an inner contradiction between the fighting woman who had dedicated herself to the struggle for the survival of her people and the woman who loved unreservedly, who had given up her freedom and the possibility of fighting further by turning herself in to the police.

In prison some of the other inmates told me that, even in her prison cell, Gusta-Justyna organized demonstrations against the Germans, continued to sing revolutionary songs, and treated with total contempt the German sadists who were torturing her.

Early in April 1943, Szymek, his conspiratorial ardor unabated, sent Gusta orders to escape from the prison. They were both fighters, and both fought passionately to preserve the honor of the Jewish people; they still dreamed of continuing the struggle against the Germans. They escaped in separate actions, but a few months later they both died at the hands of the German executioners.

→►◄←

Gusta-Justyna was a talented writer who wrote her memoir in prison, amidst inhuman conditions created by the German captors. Gusta was driven to record the fate of the Jewish resistance fighters for posterity, and thus kept on writing even while listening to the screams and groans of prisoners. She wrote her memoir on pieces of toilet paper between interrogations, during which she suffered physical and psychological torture. Despite some stylistic infelicities, her memoir is living proof of her literary talent.

JOZEF WULF
Krakow, October 1945

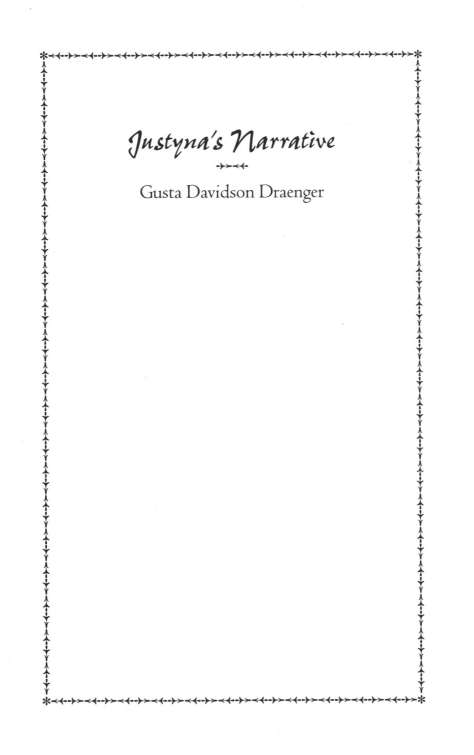

Justyna's Narrative

Gusta Davidson Draenger

Last Will & Testament

⁓⊱⊰⁓

From this prison cell that we will never leave alive, we young fighters who are about to die salute you.

We offer our lives willingly for our holy cause, asking only that our deeds be inscribed in the book of eternal memory.

May the memories preserved on these scattered bits of paper be gathered together to compose a picture of our unwavering resolve in the face of death.

⁓⊱⊰⁓

The fighters whose deeds are commemorated in this narrative were members of several Jewish youth organizations who overcame ideological differences to unite in resisting the inhuman powers of evil determined to annihilate them as a race, a religion, a culture, and a people. These organizations are:

A.H.H. Akiva
Dror Freiheit
Hashomer Hatzair
Hashomer Hadati
The Circle of Young Jewish Literati
Histadrut Hanoar Hechalutzi, known as Hechalutz[1]

---

1. The Jewish youth groups mentioned here embodied various ideologies. Akiva was Zionist center; Dror Freiheit, Zionist Labor; Hashomer Hatzair, Marxist Zionist; and Hashomer Hadati, religious Zionist.

➤►◄‹

This being my last will and testament, let whoever finds these hidden scraps after the war send them to one of the following addresses: Kibbutz Akiva, Hadera, Palestine, or Beit Yehoshua, Palestine-Hasharon.

G.D.D.

Kopaliny

-+->-<+-

THE SUN WAS SINKING behind the forest, which extended from the outskirts of the mansion into the distance like a dark stain till it fused with the blue mountains in the far-off horizon. The stillness hovering luxuriantly above the orchard spread itself across the golden fields, lay down indolently in the dense pastures, circled the mansion, and expired in the boundless forest. Summer was at its peak.

No one had returned yet from the fields. As far as the eye could see, not a soul disturbed nature's stillness with even the slightest movement. All creation seemed suspended in the heat of the summer day. In the profound silence, it was easy to forget that war was raging and blood being spilled, that violence, evil, brutality, lawlessness, human injury, and pain existed on this earth. The stillness exhaled by the deep woods floated down from the sky to be inhaled by the earth. Not so much as a single leaf quivered.

A small figure came into view, moving among the currant bushes.

"I picked a lot of currants today!" Witek called out.[2] He laughed nonchalantly, looked all around, and started to put currants into his mouth. The forest echoed his silvery, childish laughter, rendering the silence deeper still. The cuckoo bird must have grown tired, for his calls grew fainter.

---

2. Witek was Justyna's five-year-old nephew, a kind of mascot to the group who had been more or less adopted by Szymek and Gusta.

Antek was sitting under the pear tree.[3] He had just left off working in the fields and had taken a short cut across the forest. He stowed the ax and saw in the shed, then ran into the orchard and plunked himself down in the shade of the pear tree. He waited expectantly for Marek to speak, yet Marek said nothing.[4] He lay stretched out on the terrace, taut as a violin string. His head leaning on his palms, he gazed into the distance. With the crystalline sky so transparent and the mountains so distant, how far could he project his willful gaze? He seemed to have forgotten about the world, even to have forgotten the person sitting next to him, waiting for him to speak. Marek himself had summoned Antek from the forest with a message that he leave his work instantly and report for an important consultation. And now, nothing. Marek wrinkled his brow, and you could virtually see the thoughts racing furiously beneath his tanned forehead.

Both young, both muscular and robust, they remained motionless, like figures in a portrait. There was a mysterious harmony between the two young people under the pear tree in the silence. But while the somnolent summer day burst with nature's miraculous ripeness, the young men's souls were racked by a spring storm driving them to attempt another kind of miracle, a human miracle that they never succeeded in bringing to fruition.

A silhouette flitted among the trees. Justyna looked around the orchard, quickened her pace, and called from a distance, "Excuse me for having kept you waiting so long." She smiled, somewhat embarrassed. "But I have so many things to take care of, and even the smallest chore takes time."

"Hurry up and sit down," Marek replied with a hint of impatience. He looked at his watch and added, "It's late. Soon people will be coming back from the fields, and then you'll have to start rushing to get Witek to Wisnicz. And we have important matters to discuss."

When Justyna sat down without answering, Marek said in a soft voice, "Up to now we haven't held a really important meeting."

---

3. Since she was writing her memoir in prison, where it might have been found by guards, Justyna assigned aliases to the characters she was commemorating. Antek is Hillel Wodzislawski, killed in October 1943.

4. The Marek of the *Narrative* is Shimson (Szymek) Draenger, Gusta's husband and one of the leaders of the movement.

Antek and Justyna looked at him curiously, and only then noticed the peculiar depth and sharpness in his eyes. Marek got to his feet and started to speak, weighing each word.

"When I returned from Krakow this time, I came back surer than I've ever been that we're not going to survive the war." He paused as the sharp clang of his words dug into the stillness.

"We won't survive," he repeated. "At least not as a movement, not as an integral unit. Individuals may survive, but not the movement. Isolated here in the tranquility of Kopaliny, we lose touch with what is happening all around us. The mass killings are spreading across wider and wider areas. It won't be long before the fire consumes our entire people, erasing us from the earth, and none of us will have the slightest chance of escaping the devouring flames. The enemy will succeed with their diabolical plot to annihilate us.

"We didn't anticipate such unrestrained savagery. We thought the war and the occupation were a momentary tremor, and that if we could somehow manage to live through the initial shock we would find some way to survive. That's why we've kept believing we could go on living in the dream world of our grandiose ideas while the storm raged around us."

They didn't doubt Marek's words, but they were determined to remain true to their ideals to the end. They weren't blind to the truth, but they chose to keep to the path they had mapped out. Nothing could force them to deviate from it or to give up the ideals that had become a part of their beings. As time went on, the more viciously they were beaten, the firmer they became in their convictions; the more they were taunted, the more firm was their belief that they had chosen the right way. Their strongest desire was to continue being worthy of serving as the backbone of the movement, as a reservoir of strength. They wanted to light a spark in every young person, to move the youth into the vanguard and motivate them to effective action.

They hoped to counteract the spreading cynicism. People were growing more skeptical of the value of high ideals and were turning their backs on uplifting thought and action. They no longer behaved considerately and even seemed contemptuous of the human soul itself. War was robbing the young of their humanity. It was teaching them to elbow others out of their way, to push someone else into the abyss so that they might survive, to cling to life desperately and at any price, whether that price be pride, freedom, even one's own soul, which was all too often sold to the enemy without the slightest hesitation or scruple.

As in ancient times, those who were to become leaders of the movement preserved the sacred flame by fueling it with the live coals of their hearts. With those around them trapped in the quagmire of oppression, the leaders set up outposts to nurture the highest ideals. These lonely outposts would become their rock and their shield, their stay against confusion and chaos.

At first they had worked erratically, without an overall plan. The imprisonment of Marek and Justyna during the first days of the occupation and their subsequent deportation to a concentration camp in the Sudetenland had cast a pall over the incipient movement. When they returned unexpectedly three months later, having miraculously escaped the lion's jaws, the danger had not diminished.[5] For the next few months they were hounded constantly, at the mercy of blackmailers and in danger of being denounced. But outside the cordon encircling the Krakow area, the organization continued to flourish, its main operations having shifted to Vilna so that the work on Polish soil would not have to stop. Those who were able to break through the police cordon headed for Vilna, the new nerve center of the ill-fated youth movement, and it was in Vilna that the movement's ideological course was set. Yet the movement leaders knew that the conflagration would consume this last island of organized communal action as well, so under the rule of the General Government they set up alternative outposts.

Whether in Gebultow, Warsaw, Hipnitz, or Kopaliny, there was always one locale where the flame kept burning, where their vigorous traditions were preserved. When one outpost was destroyed, they immediately moved to another and started over, always with the same enthusiasm. It was not long before their chosen road was strewn with martyrs. Burdened with pain after the death of Siki, then of Lusiek, they had to consider whether to continue the work

---

5. Szymek and Gusta's first imprisonment, in 1939; Szymek was imprisoned for his anti-Fascist writings, and Gusta volunteered to join him. The episode occurred prior to their stay in Kopaliny.

when death was claiming their best workers. Disputes broke out, but a healthy attitude prevailed. The movement could not permit itself to come to a halt because of the fall of one outpost. You can't forge a fighting force without fighting. You can't try to preserve fighters by shielding them in a shelter. If you do, you will destroy their souls. Their flesh might remain intact, but their spirits would wither. What point would there be in preserving a group of fighters whose souls were not illuminated by truth, whose services were not rendered with pure motives and lit by the divine spark?

As always, they would have to let reality guide them. They decided this year to develop the movement in the Krakow region as quickly as possible by setting up and organizing agricultural outposts. They would use the time allowed by the seasonal nature of the work to strengthen their plans.

At the same time, they were working to set up a large fish-processing plant in Tomaszow-Mazowiecki with a work force of movement members. Everything was well organized and legal. The budget and finances had been set up, the plant equipped, but the day before the farm was to go into operation someone murdered their Gentile front man, who had set up everything.[6] In one night the whole plan had collapsed, and they calculated that it would not pay to begin again from scratch.

They were also organizing the Kopaliny outpost and had been planning to install a group of workers on the tobacco plantation at Tomaszow-Lubielski, which would have been supervised by Jasio. But as they were preparing to take possession of the place, a deportation order was issued that swept away the entire group of workers. Only Jasio remained, but it was not long before he too disappeared.[7]

The deportation *aktzia* in Krakow was the first of many devastat-

---

6. Since, as Jews, the movement members were not permitted by law to set up a business, they found a Pole who was willing to serve as a front man. They funded the enterprise, and he went through all the necessary legal procedures. Presumably he would have shared any profits.

7. The expulsions mentioned here probably refer to Aktion Reinhard, June 1 to June 6, 1942, when it is estimated that some 5,000 Jews were either killed on the spot or deported to Belzec. "Jasio" is the friendly Pole who served as a front man for the movement.

ing blows to the movement. Paulina and Cyla, towers of strength who had been expected to contribute significantly to building the movement, were deported. The Warsaw base, though holding its own for the time being, was nearing its end. You could hear the first rumblings of mass deportations there, so they had to start thinking about liquidating an outpost into which they had invested a great deal of effort for two years.

"Then those of us in Kopaliny will be the only ones left," said Marek. "Our days are numbered. This is the last safe place. Wherever our people live, the ground crumbles under their feet. Wherever they may be, the terror of deportation stalks them. They call it 'deportation.' Our naive people still tell themselves that the sealed cattle cars sprayed with lime are taking Jews to labor camps. On hot days and nights, crowded into wagons without windows, without air, without a drop of water, they die from suffocation. And those who arrive alive die in the gas chambers. People are submitting to this shameful death. No one resists the murderers. No one lifts a hand, or threatens them with a brandished fist. How painful it is to see thousands of women, old people, children, even men in the prime of life, let themselves be led like sheep to the slaughter. They are quiet. The world is quiet. We too have been quiet, but we won't stay quiet long. We won't let ourselves be led to the slaughter like a bunch of cattle. We won't submit our necks to the knife willingly. We will escape before the aktzia can get us. Time after time we'll swim out of the net together. They won't catch us so easily. We'll defend ourselves, and our defense will be through offense. We could just try to live through the war, to save our own skins. There are still many opportunities for personal survival at our disposal, many routes to safety. But we want to survive as a generation of avengers. If we survive, it has got to be as a group and with weapons in our hands."

Marek paused to gather his thoughts and impulsively ran his hand through his hair. A moment later he continued: "This is our decision. Dolek and Anna and I have been discussing the matter constantly. It's not as if we've come up with a new idea. This rebelliousness, this desire to regain self-respect after the shame and degradation we've had to endure, has been brewing for a long time. We've had enough debasement, enough complaining, enough limp hands. How can we do anything but resist? True, it won't be easy. They'll make us pay for every act with thousands of innocent victims. It won't be easy to exact a price for their crimes against our people, because our every move will meet with massive, indiscriminate retaliation. We can't help feeling responsible for the safety of Polish Jewry, so how could we take it upon ourselves to do anything that might result in their destruction?

"But the fate of our people on this earth has already been decided. The verdict has been sealed in the blood of millions of helpless Jews. We can either die with them or try to avenge their deaths. Our revenge will have to be pitiless and unrestrained. It will be up to us to wash away the shame of our people. We've got to forget everything we've been taught about not shedding blood, about not using force, about not resorting to the justice of the clenched fist."

Marek stood up suddenly. "It's going to be hard to leave behind everything we've created. But it was worth the effort to have cultivated our ideas, because they will bear fruit and ultimately will triumph over the hate deepening around us. Although our ideals will always remain dear to us, we don't have time now to dwell on them. Since nobody will be left to bear witness to them, we'll have to take them to the grave. But surely we won't all die. History calls us to a new path, and we will answer the summons. . . ."

The sun was already slipping below the treetops; its red luster drenched the heavens. The air grew cool as a light wind blew in from the forest. Marek was silent.

They all sat quietly, feeling no need for more words. Justyna breathed heavily. She had been waiting for this. A month ago she would have found Marek's rhetoric pompous, but today the meaning of his words struck her as crystal clear. There was no other way.

In Krakow last June, when she had lost her father and sister and had been unable to get over her sorrow, she had felt a powerful urge to attack the enemy with her bare hands. For the first time in her life she had felt that desire for revenge and that urge to strike out, even to kill. Though violence was alien to her nature, the desire kept growing, and only the strictest self-discipline kept it in check. This was her private grief: She knew who had committed the heinous deed, the culprit who deserved to have his face spit into.[8] She knew

---

8. Draenger is referring to someone who betrayed her family to the Germans or to non-German police.

the identities of those who had debased themselves. She would have no peace until she had avenged the wrongs done to her family.

[TEXT UNREADABLE]

Everybody would stick together, and from this point on their sole purpose would be to fulfill this hidden need for revenge.

It all seemed so simple. Throughout the summer heat, the fall rains, the winter storms, the spring thaw, they would remain here in the forest, using assumed names; even in pain and in hunger, they would always hold a weapon in their hands. They would avenge her father and sister, mother and brother; their friends and relatives, both distant and close; they would avenge young and old, known and unknown — all who had endured horrible deaths at the hands of the Nazis.

Antek rose, thrust his hands into his pockets, and stood for a minute, deep in thought. Then he roused himself and slapped Marek on the back.

"My brother," he said, and brandished his fist. "We'll shake them up a bit." The soldier in him had reawakened and snapped to attention.

They heard rustling in the distance. People were returning from the fields and the forest. They walked in rows with sickles and axes on their shoulders, their faces glowing with smiles.

"Witenku, come to us," they called from afar.[9] They looked the picture of health and youthful vigor as they walked together in joy. The trio under the pear tree scrutinized the procession. The sun continued sinking in the reddened sky, adding its luster to their tanned faces.

Soon these young people would be marching in file to their deaths. The agricultural tools would be gone from their shoulders. This happiness born of days spent in productive labor would disappear. They would soon be faced with a new imperative, one that would

---

9. "Witenku" is a nickname for Gusta's nephew, Witek. Those returning from the fields are members of the youth movement who have been working on the farm, receiving agricultural training. The farm was set up in Kopaliny, a village between Bochnia and Wisnicz, in December 1941.

replace the tools in their calloused hands with weapons and would hurl them into the fury of battle. Their sunny smiles would vanish, and furrows would line their foreheads. Their hands, now caked with fertile loam, would soon be soaked in blood.

The forests of Kopaliny still throbbed with a joyful hum. Radiant in the summer sun, the workers interacted animatedly. But the trio under the pear tree saw a different scene. For them, the idyllic beauty of that quiet mountain village had already been eclipsed. They already saw a new truth, a new reality.[10]

---

10. The typescript from the Ghetto Fighters Kibbutz Archive ends here. In August 1942, the farm at Kopaliny was abandoned, and the Akiba resistance moved its operations to the Krakow Ghetto, the city of Krakow, and its environs.

Krakow

→>‹←

Wʜᴇɴ Jᴜsᴛʏɴᴀ ᴀʀʀɪᴠᴇᴅ in Krakow, the machine was running in high gear. She realized this the instant she reached the Jewish Quarter.

She was worn out after a week of tribulation. For days she had been on the move constantly, waking up at the crack of dawn, walking for miles, living in a state of uninterrupted nervous tension. Those dearest to her had been in grave danger, trapped in a town surrounded by the police; since they had no way of helping themselves, it had been left to her to rescue them. First there had been Witek, then her aged mother, and finally, at the last moment, Marek's parents. Her efforts, which had exposed Justyna to continual danger, had preoccupied her for several days and left her completely exhausted. Moreover, the trip back to Krakow had been draining: the logistical difficulties of making connections, covering tens of kilometers by horse and buggy, then switching to a droshky, then to a motorcycle; the hours spent waiting in train stations; the sleepless nights; the never-ending anxiety over the safety of the loved ones whom it was her responsibility to save — each had added further to Justyna's exhaustion. Although Justyna had managed to accomplish what she had set out to do, it was now only with the greatest difficulty that she was able to force her swollen legs to drag her to the Jewish Quarter.

Justyna's face was uncharacteristically pale, and there were black circles under her eyes. She had but one desire: to collapse into bed and sleep for a week. But as she approached the barbed wire and heard the hum surging from the thickly populated streets, a wave of warmth coursed through her, dispelling her fatigue as if it were a soap bubble. Faces she recognized, faces of those close and dear, peered out at her from behind the barbed wire. She wanted to embrace them all, those she hadn't seen in almost a year and those she'd left just a week ago.[11]

Krakow was now swarming with people. A month ago the quarter had undergone a great upheaval. People had fled, scattering in all directions. Now this same quarter had become a noisy refuge to which people from towns, villages, and cities came running as if it were a safe haven. Krakow had become the main headquarters of the movement, because by this time no other place could be used as a center of operations. The most recent transports had swept away the last Jewish communities. Experience had taught people not to wait to the last minute, so now they were trying to save their lives while there was still time. As a consequence, when you met someone you recognized in the street, you were tempted to ask, "Where did you escape from?"

That was the situation. All of these people had lived through the same harrowing experiences as Justyna, escaping from one besieged city to — where? To another city that would meet the same fate in a day or two. So they ran from the village to the big city, and a few days later from the city to a small town, and when the aktzia was over, they stole back into the city again. No one doubted that escape was temporary. Still, people continued to run in circles until their strength ebbed or their money ran out, or until an aktzia took them by surprise. In the face of the relentless and certain death that stalked them, people still strove to save themselves, even though they knew that they were prolonging their lives for only another week or two. Maybe they weren't even struggling out of a desire to live, because in truth they had grown weary of so wretched an existence. They had had enough of panicked escapes. There were times when they even caught themselves secretly wishing for the end. But they wanted death to pounce on them unexpectedly, so they wouldn't have to reproach themselves for giving up. They did not want to surrender.

Even a few older people who no longer harbored any illusions

---

11. Justyna had been away from Krakow for about a week. Some of the friends greeting her had been in Krakow when she left, but others had been away on assignments or had arrived from surrounding towns within the last week.

would argue, "We're going to fall into their hands sooner or later, but we don't have to make their task any easier. Let's force them to chase us down. At least we can frustrate them a little before they snare us in their trap."

But in general the older folks lacked the fighting spirit needed to resist the enemy. But why should that come as a surprise? Anyone who has not lived through three years of degradation, humiliation, and baiting, who has not clung desperately to a life hanging by a thread in the midst of a turbulent storm, will not be able to understand the despair of these people. Only someone who has had the luxury of an unruffled existence could condemn them for having resigned themselves to their fate. If you could just see into the murkiness of their bruised, despairing souls and live a single hour in that black hopelessness, knowing that all struggle is meaningless and to no avail, knowing that there is nothing at the end of the tunnel but the ugly letters that spell out "death," then you would know what they felt, and you would say to yourself, as they said, "Let come what may" — and wait for it to happen.

It was different with the young. They clutched at life, and refused to accept their fate passively. Their powerful desire to live drove them to active resistance, which was not without its ironies, since it was this irresistible lust for life that drove them to engage an overwhelmingly superior enemy, thereby exposing themselves to certain death. Paradoxically, the perennial strength of youth was its greatest weakness. The force demanding their survival was the very force pushing them to their deaths.

The hordes fleeing deportation came streaming into Krakow. They did not yet know about the new decision. Though no letters or circulars concerning the matter had been sent out, everybody else in the immediate area had sensed that the movement would have to act and that something was afoot in Krakow.

As close friends and intimates encircled Justyna that Sunday afternoon, she realized that the quarter was where she belonged. It did not faze her in the least that she was now homeless. Having escaped deportation, she now felt secure and — ironically, given the danger — happy to be among her own. It was a warm, pleasant day; crowds of people milled in the streets, wafting the hum and buzz of their existence to the surrounding buildings. Someone escorted Justyna

46

through the narrow gate, and someone else grabbed her arms and helped her drag herself on her sore legs. She let herself be led like a young child.

She did not even recognize the particular individuals who had met her at the entrance. Their faces fused into an affectionate whole that was to remain forever fixed in her memory. She heard warm words of greeting that made her feel better than she ever felt in her life.

"We've been waiting for you desperately," a voice was saying. In truth, she did not know to whom the voice belonged.

"We've all been very worried, because we expected you on Friday, and today is Sunday."

"So many things have happened to me. The more I rushed to get here, the harder a time I had making connections. But now I'm here, and I'm about to pass out with fatigue."

New faces peered out at her from the buildings they passed.

"If you only knew how worried Marek has been! It's a pity you didn't hear the way he lashed out at Jozek and Hela.[12] He barked at them the way he does when he loses his temper. And for what? For nothing, just because he was worried. Now he'll probably calm down."

A bright blush swept over Justyna's face. It didn't surprise her that Marek worried about her two-day delay, but she hadn't expected people to be gossiping about it. She laughed loudly to conceal her embarrassment and was still laughing awkwardly when Marek made his way toward her through the crowd. Informed of her arrival, he had managed to tear himself away from his work for a minute to greet her.

Feeling the pressure of his hard, narrow palm as they stood facing each other, Justyna intuited everything immediately. It had been no accident that the responsibility for the whole family, for both mothers and for Marek's father and Witek, had fallen entirely to her. She now realized that she would be alone in this difficult time, that she would have to depend on her own strength, agility, and inventiveness. It had all grown clear to her in an instant: Marek's personal

---

12. Jozek is Jozef Wulf, one of the Akiba leaders in the Bochnia district and author of the "Introduction to the Polish Edition, 1945," which has been reprinted in this book.

life had come to an end. He was obsessed with the cause, and from now on that was the only thing that would have any meaning for him. Everyone else would have to be subordinate to that femme fatale. As Justyna looked at the features cast in bronze around his steely blue eyes, she perceived clearly that he no longer saw her, that he was seeing beyond her into the distant future, seeing those things fated to happen, concentrating on what had to take first priority in his life.

"I have only a moment to spare," he said. Justyna knew very well that he was going to say something like that, and that from now on he would never be able to spare more than a moment for her.

"Did you take care of everyone? Is everything in order?"

"Everything went fine."

"How come it took you so long to get back? I was terribly worried that something bad had happened."

"A lot did happen to me. There's so much I want to tell you."

"Right, right. I want to know everything, but right now I can only spare a minute." He leaned over, close to her ear: "I have to go to a meeting now. You understand, don't you? Later on, this evening, I'll stop by to see you and we'll have a chat. Right now, you should get some rest."

As they passed a yellow apartment building, Marek whistled a short signal. Dolek leaned out of the first-floor window.[13]

"She made it," Marek said, pointing to Justyna.

The two men smiled warmly at each other across the distance; they said nothing. That's probably where the meeting will be, Justyna thought. Thinking of those deliberations, which loomed so large in her imagination yet seemed so distant and unattainable, she was overcome by profound feelings of an almost religious reverence. Having belonged to the movement for several years, she had been present at some of the weightiest discussions, and it had been a long time since she had been intimidated by the thought of a mere meeting, no matter how important. But at this moment, she was overwhelmed by a consciousness of her own insignificance.

She asked sheepishly, "Is this where the meeting will be?"

---

13. Dolek is Aharon Liebeskind, one of the leaders of the movement.

Marek didn't answer. Somebody was standing close enough to overhear, so he just winked knowingly. A thought flashed through Justyna's mind: Conspiracy! How different everything has become these days.

-+->-<+-

How long had it been since Dolek last visited Wisnicz? Maybe a couple of weeks. He had arrived a few days after the camp in Kopaliny had been overrun. They had recalled Dolek to Krakow because they realized as soon as the Kopaliny farm was lost that they would have to rebuild a base of operations either here or in the vicinity. When Dolek got to Krakow, he put the Kopaliny farm incident into perspective.

"There's nothing to be sorry for," he said. "The Kopaliny farm was a dream we had to wake up from. It could have lasted another week, maybe two. But it had to end sometime. So what's there to be sorry about? Those two weeks? My dear friends, in a month you won't be able to find any trace of communities that have been in existence for hundreds of years, communities with roots deep in this soil. So let's remember our beautiful and creative summer joyfully. Who knows, it may have been our last."

Hearing Dolek's words, Justyna recalled that wonderful summer in Kopaliny. Those beautiful, deeply blue and silent mornings when they would stroll along the ridges, then walk down the ravine that sloped gently toward the stream. Only the clanging of reapers' scythes could be heard in the distance, while an uninterrupted tranquility floated above the cut stalks of wheat. Sitting on the grass, the four of them — Antek, Dolek, Marek, and Justyna — vowed that they would dedicate their entire beings to the cause. There was no point in trying to hold on to a dead past or to a world that was quickly disappearing. They had to live each day as it came. Who could say what tomorrow might bring?

The only thing certain for them was that there was no tomorrow. They vowed that for as long as life went on, even if only for a single day, they would strive to create. Then the reality of their situation would suddenly crash in on their dreams: "My God! Create? Destroy, destroy, destroy — with every ounce of strength left in us! Because for us the only creativity must be destruction. For us that is the only thing still worth living for. Everything else will pass. Only what we have destroyed will remain."

How paradoxical! They who were young and strong and still had the power to build a just world, they who had spent every day of their lives enacting their belief in human justice, must now consecrate their lives through bloodshed, through guerrilla activities, sabotage, subversion, destruction, and extermination.

In her mind's eye she saw the reapers mowing with calm, smooth strokes, bending and straightening, while the sun rolled slowly through the azure sky.

→>-◄-

Now, only two weeks after that idyllic scene, they have reached another stage in the struggle. In Kopaliny they were still deciding how to proceed, but now the work has started. Maybe not the work itself, but at least the preparations for it. The planning is still going on, not in grassy meadows and harvested fields, but closeted within four conspiratorial walls. Justyna doesn't know just how far the planning has come, but she knows things are in motion. When Marek returns this evening, maybe she'll be able to get some information out of him. Right now, however, she must go home obediently.

As she is ruminating, somebody embraces her. It is Hanka, known as "Sister Anna," a motherly type who dedicates herself to caring for the suffering and the oppressed.[14]

"Your legs are swollen," she observes immediately. "Take off those heavy shoes and put on my wooden clogs, and do it quickly!" They are standing in the middle of the street, blocking traffic, because Hanka is determined that Justyna must change her footgear.

"Now let's go home and get you right to bed. You're so worn out you look as if you've been crucified."

"My dear Hanusha, it's been almost a year since I've seen you!"

---

14. Hanka is Hannah Spritzer, a trained nurse who frequently took care of the wounded. Deported to Auschwitz, 19 January 1943.

Justyna bursts out. "You haven't changed at all, though you've gotten awfully emaciated!"

They are so happy to see each other that they both try to talk at the same time, their questions and answers overlapping as they trade affectionate glances.

Various people approach Justyna and shake her hand. Greetings and good wishes are exchanged, but not everybody realizes that these meetings are taking place at a fateful juncture of eras, with one ending and the other just about to begin.

→>-<-

The days flew by and Marek did not return. Those days of waiting for him were the worst; they were nightmarish. Lying in bed and thinking that Marek should have been back by then, Justyna began to perceive the magnitude of the task they had undertaken. Not that they were the first among humankind to take up arms with the purpose of abolishing the established order. In ages past, as recorded in the annals of history, a handful of madmen were always ready to take up their pitchforks and go marching into the sun to meet death head-on.

The activists in the movement were all young, so it seemed natural for them to choose the path of revolution. But the fact that they were also Jews in these times tended to make their revolutionary ideals into mere chimeras. This, then, was their dilemma: they longed eagerly to join the general struggle for the betterment of humankind, but because they were Jews, they had no choice but to devote every ounce of their strength and energy to the struggle for their own survival.

To understand their plight, you would have to imagine what life must have been like in the Middle Ages — what it means for a human being to have the severest restrictions imposed upon him, to be stripped of all hope in life, to be removed from all the trappings of the civilized world, to be locked up in a barbed wire cage and told, "Sit here and wait for the death we are devising for you." Maybe during the Middle Ages the condemned were unconscious of the noose being drawn tighter and tighter around their necks until it strangled them completely. But we have to go on clawing to survive, while fully aware that nothing can possibly save us from the fate to which we have been condemned so unjustly. Who in this world has ever been faced with so many prohibitions, so many ordinances, so many rules whose violation is punishable by death! In truth, death sentences are inflicted without the least provocation, and anyone who tries to defy these unjust laws, to defend his life or stand up for his inalienable human rights, is sentenced to a death even more horrible than the one he could expect in the normal course of events. Anyone who leaves the ghetto walls earns a death sentence. Anyone who appears on the streets without a white and blue armband is subject to a death sentence. Anyone who walks onto a trolley car, a horse-drawn carriage, a train, or a bus earns a death sentence.

You don't have to be a revolutionary to risk a death sentence. Just being yourself and making one false move is enough to trigger one of the many traps set to ensnare Jews.

In the ghetto, your choice is either to die or to wait passively for deportation to some unknown destination that would lead eventually to the gas chamber. Anybody who wants to resist first has to leave the ghetto — and it is precisely here that one takes on the most difficult struggle.

It is very easy to say, "Just run away before they deport you!" But how do you manage to sneak out of a ring of barbed wire surrounded and closely guarded by police? How do you take your first step into the outside world? They will see the armband on your sleeve, and you can be certain that a bullet to your head will follow. Should you remove the armband? As soon as someone notices that white symbol sliding down your sleeve, he will betray you and deliver you into the hands of the police. Then perhaps you should try to slip into the blackness of the darkest doorway, and there undertake to remove the ornament adorning your arm. No matter how dark that doorway, there will always be someone who notices that you stepped into it a Jew and stepped out as if you were a human being. Why "as if you were a human being"? Because to take off the armband successfully, you first have to regain your sense of human dignity. Without that, you are nothing more than a Jew without an armband.

You would reveal your Jewishness in a thousand small ways: every anxiety-filled move; every step taken with a back hunched over from the yoke of slavery; every glance that bespoke the terror of a hunted animal; the entire form, the face on which the ghetto had left its indelible mark. You were nothing more than a Jew, not only because of the color of your eyes, hair, skin, the shape of your nose, the many telltale signs of your race. You were simply and unmistakably a Jew because of your lack of self-assurance, your way of expressing yourself, your behavior, and God knows what else. You were simply and conspicuously a Jew because everybody outside the ghetto strained to detect your Jewishness, all those people eager to do you harm, who couldn't abide the thought that you might be cheating death. At your every step they would look straight into your eyes — impudently, suspiciously, challengingly — until you would become entirely confused, turn beet red, lower your eyes — and thus show yourself to be undeniably a Jew.

By the time you made it to the railroad station you had already absorbed a series of beatings administered by prying eyes, wordless questions inflicted by the enemy lurking in every passerby, chance encounters with outright hoodlums. By the time you got to the railroad station you had drained so much from your emotional reserves that you barely had enough left to get you to the next town. By the time you finally arrived at the railroad station you had so eagerly longed to reach, you found yourself under the close scrutiny of organized terror. All sorts of police would be milling around with the sole purpose of ferreting out disguised Jews. Secret police, Germans, Ukrainians, and every variety of Fascist were now in control. You had to be very cold-blooded to get yourself to walk through the station with your head held high, to flash back the impertinent stares of the secret police, and then to step calmly onto the railroad car. Now that the rabble was in control, they no longer had to worry about being subtle. Everybody was scrutinized. No sooner was a Jew sniffed out than he was turned over to the police. Otherwise he would have to cough up all his money to blackmailers who threatened to give away his secret. And even after he had done so, he would be threatened and terrorized till his spirit was completely broken, and he would long for death as the only escape from total humiliation.

If with the utmost expenditure of nervous energy you were able to deceive your would-be tormentors, then you were condemned to eavesdrop on highly unpleasant conversations about Jews that would make your blood boil. The talk would go something like this: "It's high time they get what's coming to them. They're getting no more than they deserve. Many tried to escape, but luckily they were caught. They were trying to hoard all the gold, but it was taken from them just in the nick of time . . ." It was mean talk, malicious lies. But most appalling was the primitive, bestial joy the speakers displayed at the thought that hundreds of thousands of women, children, and elderly were dying! They waited like hyenas for the victims to perish so they could rob and plunder them, take over their abandoned houses, inherit the spoils.

In the corner of the coach, listening to these calumnies, sits a human being who has still not recovered from the loss of those dearest to him. And yet he dare not let a single muscle on his face so much as twitch, for should he betray any excitement or pain — aha! — surely he must be a Jew. Inside, his blood is boiling, but outside he wears a mask of stone. Should he permit himself to betray his emotions for even a fraction of a second, he is lost.

Anyone who has survived one of those trips could enlighten the world about the trials of Odysseus. For Gentiles, a train trip was an uncomfortable experience, but for a Jew every step outside the barbed wire was like passing through a hail of bullets. It was like standing at the front line of a battle. The only thing that could save you was chance, chance and inner strength. To develop that toughness, you had to put yourself through a psychological ordeal, from which you would emerge either pure and high-principled or base and depraved. Since the path was so narrow and slippery, many plunged into the abyss of degradation. It was easy to falter and start feeling contempt for yourself! For millennia Jews had stood up to those who had dared insult them. Could they now so lower themselves as to deny the Jewishness they had proudly carried through the ages in their very names? Could those who had sacrificed their carefree youths for the sake of a Jewish renascence and who had sought the meaning of life in their Jewishness now alienate themselves from that very Jewishness by cringingly concealing their origins?

Without that inner toughness, the resistance fighters would not have been able to take a single step forward. After struggling against the rumblings of inner rebellion that would make them want to drop their protective armor and challenge the rabble on the spot, they would manage to maintain a stony composure. But that did not mean they were denying their Jewish identities. They would do anything to accomplish their purpose, and any action or evasion that served to bring about the ultimate goal became sacred. In deciding not to reveal their Jewish identities at some moments, they were executing a strategic retreat that would enable them to regroup and counterattack at the time and place of their choosing. The deeper inside they buried their Jewish identities, the more intensely Jewish they felt. The more they humbled themselves on the outside, the prouder they became. They were never more conscious of their Jewishness than when concealing it, and there was never a doubt that they would remain Jews until their very last moments. Not for an instant did they think that they would not be standing at the edge of an abyss if they weren't Jews. The fact that they could not admit their Jewishness in these torturous instances intensified their determination. They believed their moment of triumph would come, but in order to bring it about they had to carry on their struggle underground.

This self-denial was a transitional phase, a necessary condition of Jewish resistance. Other underground fighters had to conceal their resistance activities and everything related to them, but the Jewish fighters had to mask every part of themselves — their origins, appearances, customs, mentalities, ideas, even their Jewish souls, which had been nurtured painstakingly through the centuries. Only when they had succeeded in effacing the essence of their beings could they start planning underground activities. Will anyone ever be able to comprehend how this group of idealistic dreamers took up arms, in spite of being deprived of the right to live as human beings and as Jews, denied even the right to eat? All you had to do to fall into a trap was to show up on the street, without any weapons or subversive intentions. Will anyone ever understand the revolutionary's fear of slipping up before he even sets out on his mission, or the freedom fighter's fear of dying before achieving his goal? None of them feared death itself, but all dreaded the possibility of falling into the hands of the authorities for some trifling matter unrelated to the movement's work. They wanted to die with dignity, to go down fighting, not to die a trivial death.

They found that assuming another character — becoming the right type, wearing the right clothes — took up a large part of their daily preparations for launching subversive activities. Facial expressions and "typical Aryan" features became matters of such importance that physical appearance began to influence the way people calculated human worth. What you looked like took precedence over who you were. If you didn't have the right look, it did not matter how strong and courageous you were. But the fighters found a way to deal even with this problem. Their youthful pride and confidence in their cause helped them. The ghetto had not succeeded in putting the stamp of slavery onto their fresh faces. They left the Jewish Quarter with heads held high, walked with a firm, elastic step, and conducted themselves with such self-assurance as to force others to yield. No one who saw their demeanor could imagine them as prey stalked by a predator; no one dared to humiliate or insult them. But their impregnability hung by a thread. Just one memory, one reflection, would suffice to lower the head momentarily, to mist the eyes, to bring a strange melancholy to the face, and then the imprint of the oppressed Jew would emerge for all to see. At a moment like this nothing could save such a person — not his fair hair or gray eyes, not even his turned-up nose — because his suffering Jewish soul had emerged in all its splendor, and there was nothing the fighter could do to suppress it!

So despite the self-assurance and swagger of the Jewish resistance fighters, they remained vulnerable: it was impossible for them to eradicate every trace of Jewish identity. How many were the beautiful young women who attracted attention with their exotic good looks! Even if they bleached their curly black braids, their Jewishness and their unusual Semitic beauty would still be apparent through the haunting expression in their deep, dark eyes. Danger lurked at every turn, at every trolley stop. Here an old acquaintance, there a hooligan, somewhere else a detective, once more a policeman with penetrating eyes, and finally a body search. In short, every path was an obstacle course, every street a dense jungle that had to be cleared with a machete. The entire experience of the Jewish resistance fighters was an uncharted voyage. Never before had it been necessary for them to play such roles. They were accustomed to leading honest, straightforward lives. So first, even before engaging the enemy in battle, they had to win the inner struggle to transform themselves, and the price of losing that struggle was usually death.

Once you had taken on the role, you had to see it through to the very end. How many times in the hands of the police did you have to lie and deny your Jewishness to the bitter end? But oh, how much fortitude was required to do it!

Most often one's nerves gave out, snapping like taut strings. In those crucial moments, a desperate thought would come to mind: "I lived as a Jew, and as a Jew I will die." Sometimes, just as the words of confession had forced themselves to the victim's lips, an inner voice would command him to save himself one more time for the good of the cause, and then the strained nerves would slacken at the thought of the ultimate victory. One's fate in most such incidents, however, was decided by some fortuitous accident, and in these instances one can hardly claim a victory.

→►◄←

Justyna is worried because Marek has not yet returned. True, they had gotten a telegram from him yesterday, but so many things could have happened since then. It did not take hours for catastrophe to strike: one second was enough, a mere blink of an eye, and all was lost. Someone might glance at him and think, "I know this person," and that would be the end of him.

Is it only as he is leaving the apartment of our contact in Lvov that he is in danger of being apprehended? Would the authorities have to find a concealed weapon or incriminating papers on him? No. All they would have to do is sniff him out, discover that he is a Jew.

In a split second, in the blink of an eye, it would be all over.

Justyna buries her head under the quilt, trying to escape the gloomy thoughts she cannot force out of her mind.

No! Marek will never surrender. He won't slip up. He has already walked through fire many times; he has been hardened by constant exposure to danger. In the three years since the war broke out, he hasn't known a moment's peace. His incessant travels under the most difficult conditions have sharpened his reflexes and stretched his powers of endurance. He is not likely to be taken by surprise. Whatever happens, Marek will make it through.

To quiet her jangled nerves, Justyna brings to mind those poor souls without Marek's savvy, who take to the road totally unprepared, oblivious to the perils that await them. Their prospects of returning are slim to nil, yet they set out on their journey without hesitation. They go courageously, never weighing the consequences. If Justyna should worry about anyone, it should be these simple souls who hurl their *morituri te salutant* with a joy that sometimes makes you think they are children who do not grasp the full gravity of their situation. Yet every one of them has lived through hell. Every one has had at least one brush with death.

"My God," thought Justyna, "how much energy we've spent so far, and how little we've accomplished. If the effort it took to get together in Krakow just to proclaim our readiness to fight had been spent fighting the enemy, we might have won many battles by now. We've been through such an ordeal, yet we've barely begun.

"Gathered at this mobilization point, we await our orders. Soon enough we'll have to face the grim reality that's in store. If we accomplish no more than what we have already, won't that be enough? If our deeds are measured by the strenuousness of our efforts, then our struggles will be vindicated. After all, resisting tyranny in itself is worthwhile. Confounding the enemy, even temporarily, will bring us some satisfaction."

Justyna recalled a conversation she'd had with Marek when the deportations had begun.

"We ought to go from city to city," he said, "to alert people that there is no such thing as deportation, only a death sentence. They shouldn't delude themselves into believing it's safer to stay where they are than to run. They should try to escape while they still have the chance. And they should leave all at once and overwhelm the trains, the roads, the whole country. Think how much more difficult we could make things for the enemy. It's true that the hunt would then turn into a mass slaughter, but what's that to us? We'll all die anyway. They would have to deal with a full-scale revolution. They would be up to their elbows in muck.

"At the end they wouldn't know what they were doing any more. They would lose their ability to distinguish Jews from non-Jews. It would get harder and harder to segregate Jews from the rest of the populace, and their frustration would deepen. Every act of sedition would diminish their strength and disrupt their order."

"Listen," Justyna replied. "Do you really believe that even a successful uprising would have more than symbolic significance? Do you think that our rebellion could possibly influence the overall political situation?"

"Without a doubt. After all, we're not alone in this. Sparks are ready to ignite in every country. If a fire can be lit in one, the flames will sweep across Europe. We will be one link in a chain of fire that will cleanse the world. You can only get rid of this evil by digging it out at the roots. Our participation is as important as any other nation's."

"This is the music of the distant future," said Justyna sadly.

"Oh no, absolutely not. A new world is not that far off. Look, a well-organized underground army is fighting in Yugoslavia. That army has accomplished a lot, but they can't defeat the enemy by themselves. They should not be left to struggle in isolation. Everyone alive who still possesses a human soul should follow in the steps of that heroic underground army. If all those who believe in a just world would rebel, the enemy forces would fall into ruin. Think! Our destiny is in our hands! Think how likely success would be, if only all of the oppressed said this to themselves!"

Whenever thoughts crowd Justyna's mind like this, she grows restless. Her body can't stay idle; she can't sit around empty-handed, with so many tasks begging to be done.

"Tomorrow I'll get up," she decides. "Enough rest. I must get to work."

→►◄←

The next day, Justyna was completely recovered. She rose early and busied herself about the house, but nothing she did gave her any satisfaction. She still hadn't managed to find a direction for her new life that would give it significance. Friends came to visit again, and once again they all went out into the streets. Though she enjoyed their company, something within her remained unfulfilled.

She was sitting at Witek's bedside one evening when someone burst in unexpectedly with the news that Marek was stuck outside the walls of the ghetto.[15]

---

15. After June 1942, Jews were not allowed to enter or leave the ghetto without a

Justyna was alone in the house with Witek, so there was nobody she could send to help Marek get in. Finally her sister-in-law came by, and she took Tadek's pass and went to see what she could do. A quarter of an hour passed, and then another. It was almost curfew time, and no one had returned. Justyna's patience was running out. Her worst nightmare had long been that Marek would survive a long, dangerous trip only to run into trouble at the very last instant, just before he could get back into the ghetto. She was pacing the floor, trying to calm her nerves, when the door opened and Marek walked in.

"You're alone?" Justyna asked in surprise, trying to suppress a tremor that wanted to force itself into her throat.

"Of course I'm alone. No one came to get me."

"That's impossible. I sent Irena. Mietek, too. And I think somebody else might have gone to meet you."

"I didn't see anyone."

"So how did you get in?"

"When I saw that it was almost nine o'clock, I figured there was no use waiting any longer, so I scaled the wall and jumped inside."

"Madness," thought Justyna. But since she didn't want to ruin their reunion, she asked simply, "How was it?"

"I'll tell you the whole story tomorrow. I just wanted to check in. Right now I have to go to Dolek's. I'll be back early tomorrow."

When he left, Justyna was overcome with sadness. She couldn't decide whether it was better to be separated physically from Marek and to imagine that they would be reunited spiritually on his return, or to be physically close yet spiritually distant.

After Marek returned from Lvov, the fighters intensified their efforts to get things going. They believed they would have to venture out into the forest, but the forest was a mystery to them. Since none of them had ever been there, the forest remained a complete unknown. How did the people there manage to survive? What kind of lives did they lead? Everyone knew that something big was happening there, that a momentous battle was being planned, and everyone was eager to participate, though autumn was approaching and con-

---

special permit. Points of entry and exit were patrolled by German guards, Polish police, and Jewish police (*Ordnungsdienst*).

ditions would not be ideal. Did the enthusiasm driving these young people to an unknown wilderness constitute a true readiness for battle, or was it simply another instance of their youthful romanticism? Each person had to make his or her own decision, but anyone who made the decision to go became a better person in the process, a purer self that exuded an aura of heroism.

They organized into groups of five in keeping with the underground resistance blueprint, which called for each group of five members to be set up as a self-sufficient unit, with its own leader, communications expert, administrator, and supply officer. Each unit was to have its own weapons, provisions, operating area, and independent plan of action. In short, each unit would be enclosed in its own world, its own life, and would be responsible for its own operations. It was of utmost importance that only other members should know its members and its plans. But even within each unit, no one dared inquire where one of the other members would be going or when, or even where the others were at any moment.

It now became the highest obligation of individual conspirators to shield the founders of the movement, who were its cadre. This policy of secretiveness created great anxiety among the conspirators, because the demands of a secret military organization were in direct contradiction to the ideals that had nourished the movement in the past. They had been a youth movement completely dedicated to nonviolence and cultural activities and now, practically overnight, they had to make this tremendous leap of transforming a nonviolent cultural group into a military organization.

Their consciousness of the imminence of death intensified their emotions. Nearly everyone had lost home and family. The group had become the last refuge on their mortal journey, the last port for their innermost feelings, to which they now clung with all their might. The more their faith in humanity was diminished by the spreading violence and humiliation, the stronger their faith grew in each other, to the exclusion of all else. They loved one another with a unique devotion.

They met in groups often, since they were constantly seeking each other out. Their laughter and ease made it unlikely that they would go unnoticed. Countless times they were warned not to gather in groups, and on countless occasions they had actually decided, "We won't congregate anymore." Yet no sooner did two meet than others would start joining them, and soon they would all be walking down the street, their hair blowing in the wind, their faces bright and candid, their postures straight, their steps firm. Bystanders watched them pass, and you could never be sure what these people were thinking or what they might be plotting. The fighters knew their behavior was not prudent, but when they were together they felt so invulnerable that they feared no enemy. Their brazenness was surely a sin of youth, but who could condemn them, and who would want to dampen their joy in living? Their displays of exuberance provided a desperate outlet for their prematurely scarred psyches. If someone were to ask whether they might be too immature to be effective movement fighters, then what answer could one give, since they had never had the chance to experience youth at all and never would?

The movement's administration, actively engaged as never before, was located in the heart of the Jewish Quarter, though it should have been concealed far from the ghetto. Common sense dictated that the leadership not be centralized, that the leaders have separate, secret dwellings far apart, and that they meet only to discuss urgent business. They lived among people who had known them for many years, any of whom could point and proclaim, "These are the leaders of the Jewish fighting youth!"

There were four leaders: Dolek, Romek, Marek, and Maniek.[16] Since Maniek, the youngest, was somewhat of an outsider, the remaining trio actually comprised the backbone of the movement. Dolek and Marek had been close friends for many years. They had overcome many obstacles together and had lived through many ups and downs in the movement, even seen it come close to collapse. They knew each other intimately and complemented each other well, though at times they did have serious differences. On fundamentals, however, and in their ideals, they were of one mind, especially now, when the youth movement found itself at a critical juncture.

Romek was a newcomer who represented a splinter group that

---

16. Romek was Abraham Leibowicz, also known as Laban. Maniek was Maniek Eisenstein, killed on March 20, 1943.

held divergent views. At inter-party gatherings prior to the forma-
tion of the resistance movement, the three men discovered that their
groups had significant ideological differences. But when the three
came together now to assume the responsibility of leading the youth
insurrection, the differences that had kept them apart melted away,
making them feel as if they had been partners for years and had
never disputed each others' convictions.

Tall and broad-shouldered, Romek was candid in his dealings
with others and had an inexplicable charisma that instantly generated feelings of warmth in those around him. It seemed as if he had
not a care in the world, as if nothing could frighten or ruffle him.
And he looked at things so cool-headedly and saw everything with
such realism that he was able to sense the fine line between the comic
and the tragic; he could see the humor in any situation. Romek had a
uniquely Jewish sense of humor that could make life seem comical
and pleasant even in the most desperate conditions.

People clung to him and wanted to be with him whenever possible. The better they got to know him, the more they liked him. The
three principal leaders, and you could even say all four of them,
spent every spare moment together and worked in total harmony.
People clustered around them in droves, each choosing one as father,
guardian, and friend—in short, as a surrogate for all the Germans
had torn away. The leaders opened new horizons to their followers,
giving a useful direction to their pent-up energies by putting them to
work for the movement.

How then could the leaders separate from their followers and
insulate themselves in a cozy hiding place? To whom would the
rank and file run with their despair, pain, and uncertainty? Always
acutely aware of their positions as leaders of a youth movement,
they felt themselves spiritually bound to their followers. They had
total faith in each other; each had no doubt that any would rather
die than betray a friend. They were used to making all decisions by
consensus, whether trivial or important; no one would take it upon
himself to make a decision that endangered the fighters' lives.

They perceived their conspiracy as a necessary evil, a path they
would not have chosen under normal conditions but to which they
could see no alternative. In fact, they felt an aversion to conspiratorial movements, feeling that conspiracy often became an end in

itself rather than the means toward a nobler goal. Those who engaged in conspiracy for its own sake, they felt, nursed the delusion that because they operated in secret, they must be doing something significant. Since the movement leaders considered these conspirators all the more hypocritical for hiding under a mantle of idealism, they desperately wanted to prevent their movement from falling into such self-delusion. So why were they so obsessed with concealing their own work? They told themselves that the secrecy was a temporary measure, that they had to go underground to get the work started. Hence, when the groups of five were organized, the leaders believed that they were setting in motion the means toward a higher end. Meanwhile, they made the best of their situation by fully enjoying each other's company. Their dwellings were always overflowing with movement people.[17]

Marek was the first to engage in creating a conspiracy. He was assigned to organize the technical bureau, without which nothing could be undertaken. Its function was to secure freedom of movement for the conspirators. The age they lived in was one of papers, clutter, stamps, passes, certifications — in short, theirs was a time when it was impossible to leave the house without a bundle of documents. What to do, then, if you happened to be a Jew? You had to be able to show every conceivable document to prove you were not a Jew. It wasn't enough merely to have pride and self-assurance. In this time and place, the laws changed arbitrarily from day to day; each day you were required to show a different set of papers. Most importantly, you had to be able to show proof that you were employed.

The leaders of the movement had to find a way to ease the passage of Jewish fighters into and out of the ghetto. There were of course those whose racial features were so evident that no physical disguise could cover up their Jewishness. It was necessary to secure free movement for such typical Jews by supplying them with appropriate documents. This presented an enormous challenge, but since Marek was an amateur typesetter experienced in etching and engraving, he managed the task handsomely, with the courageous help of Czesiek.[18]

-----

17. Our impression is that the groups of five had been designated, but that the youths did not live in groups of five until they were on assignment.

18. Czesiek was Juda Tannenbaum, aka Idek.

Small in stature, alert, and well liked for his humorous disposition, Czesiek enjoyed access to all sorts of people. He numbered among his acquaintances not only many workers in government offices, but also some who worked in the police station, and they all trusted him. Everywhere he went, people considered him one of their own. In the Jewish Quarter he was regarded with some suspicion, for fear that he might be a double agent. People of weak character tried to ingratiate themselves with him and constantly asked him to use his influence on their behalf. Sometimes he did help. He resolved many complex problems and was able to get people into and out of the Jewish Quarter from the moment it was set up. He was bosom buddies with all the police officers, every one of whom owed him favors.[19] His popularity with bureaucrats would have made him obnoxious, were it not for the fact that he had decided to use it to serve the cause. To their surprise, movement members soon discovered that Czesiek was a man of resolute courage. Hitherto known as a prankster, a writer of journalistic schoolboy humor, and an entertaining accordionist, Czesiek turned out to be one of the most courageous ghetto fighters. He balked at nothing. He would walk into a government office casually and shake hands with the *Wachmeister*[20] with one hand while the other was unobtrusively removing government forms, schedules, and even official stamps from his desk. Taking advantage of his wide network of friends, he could buy things in stores that they didn't ordinarily sell to civilians.

Even the leaders wondered among themselves how to explain the change that had come over Czesiek. Until recently he had not shown the least interest in the movement. Since he had always behaved like a clown who was capable of little more than orchestrating amusing evenings, no one considered him capable of anything serious. Now they couldn't figure out whether he was simply living in a fool's paradise or was aware of the danger and was willing to risk being shot out of devotion to the cause. Given his past behavior, it was difficult to believe the latter. But late one evening, Czesiek delivered a monologue that one would hardly have expected from the lips of

---

19. Czesiek, that is, was able to obtain favors from the Jewish officials and the Jewish police.

20. Sergeant of the guard

the incorrigible clown he had been so recently. He had just helped two people get out of the Quarter and was escorting Justyna home. Since it was already past the nine-o'clock curfew, there was no one in the streets to overhear, so nothing prevented him from speaking his mind.

"I have to tell you something," he blurted out in a voice full of emotion, "that I've wanted to say to all of you for a long time. I know you probably won't believe what I'm about to say, and I know that my past behavior hasn't been very admirable. I've kept aloof from you all, but I've always had a great affection for everyone in the movement. There was a time when we Krakow Jews weren't doing anything constructive. We weren't progressive and just lived in the past. But frankly, I don't consider that living. I'm not a sentimental person, so I made jokes about everything, and when I couldn't ridicule something I just stood aside. But a new world is dawning. How I've longed for a life without constraints, without false scruples! Now I feel I have the chance to live up to my potential. Wherever you send me, I'll go. Sometimes you must think I'm a madman, especially when I bring things back that would earn me a bullet in the head right on the spot if I got caught with them. I do it out of my devil-may-care disposition, but don't think I don't know what's going on. I know precisely what I'm doing. I know I could be killed any minute, but as long as I'm alive I want to do what I can."

Justyna was so stunned by his sincere declaration that she was at a loss for words. Czesiek had never spoken at such length in so serious a vein. She felt obliged to tell the others what Czesiek had confided to her, because she knew that he would never be capable of such a confession again. While she was bidding Czesiek goodnight, she thought to herself that tomorrow she would repeat his confession to Marek and Dolek and the rest, but it turned out that she never told anyone. Czesiek carried on with his work. He collected whatever he could, even stealing some items as a last resort. Marek knew how to put Czesiek's booty to practical use. The two would rejoice over every new haul.

It wasn't long before the technical bureau was operating efficiently, making use of all resources. As far as Marek was concerned, what he needed most was more space. At first, he carried the whole office in his coat pockets. When something had to be done, they would first have to search furiously for a room. Once they had found it, Marek laid his tools out on a tablecloth and worked until he heard steps on the stairs. The entire office would then disappear into his pockets. When the door opened, a most innocent-looking man would be sitting at the table, reading a newspaper. But eventually Marek could no longer stuff all of the equipment into his pockets, so he started carrying a briefcase.

Marek would stroll through the ghetto carrying his briefcase, stopping in various apartments whose occupants were out. He could work out of his briefcase in his temporary headquarters until the occupant returned. He never worked in any one apartment for more than a half-hour at a time. He often disappeared into a bathroom with his little "office" and emerged half an hour later with his work completed. His dear friends used to make jokes about him. Marek and his floating office were symbolic of the movement, which started from nothing, with no outside help, and had to achieve virtually everything by dint of perseverance and will. After a while, two briefcases stuffed to capacity could no longer contain the office. The "office supplies" had increased so much that Marek was walking around with a train of assistants behind him, carrying the briefcases, boxes, a typewriter, and a variety of packages. This haphazard and exposed manner of operation put Marek at serious risk.

The incessant moving around made it harder and harder for Marek to work by himself. Since there was no secure place to leave the equipment at night, the whole caravan had to start its daily peregrinations very early in the morning. And since it was impossible to know who might drop into an apartment unexpectedly and see the now-extensive workshop in operation, each temporary headquarters was in jeopardy. Marek and those who helped carry his office around were always in grave danger.

As long as the movement fighters remained in the ghetto, preparing for but not yet engaged in combat, the dangers they faced were not so great as those they would face once they had provoked the enemy to hunt them down. Only Marek risked being caught red-handed at any moment. He was the one lugging around the blank forms, the official stamps, and all of the other telltale evidence that could have condemned him to death. For Marek and for the bureau, the danger was deadly serious. It became essential to find a permanent and well-hidden place where someone could always be on the premises. This was where Justyna's work began.

[BREAK IN THE TEXT][21]

He had run away from work, from home, from everywhere. The only place he could go was the forest, where he could finally be himself. Benek went with him.[22] A veteran of the military, Benek was once reported killed in action. But he showed up two months later, after having been a prisoner of war. For a while he was extremely depressed and avoided all contact with people. By the summer of 1942, he had started to come out of his shell. Working for the government as a manager, he began to organize a farming community. He wanted to hire his own people so he would have a congenial group to work with on the farm. Since his position was secure, he might have been able to last through the war on the farm, but when the command "To the forests!" was given, he approached Dolek immediately and told him, "I'm ready!"

Edwin went later.[23] A student of Marek's, he would have been a valuable asset to the movement were it not for his consuming ambition, which pushed him to take on tasks beyond his natural ability. Because he felt he had to prove himself at least equal to the very best, he first became Marek's disciple, then Dolek's. He couldn't understand that he was far more valuable just being himself — which is to say being a brave, sensible, and affectionate lad. Nobody doubted his capacities. In fact, the movement relied on him to do serious work. In recent years he had been counted on as one of the workers who would rebuild the movement in the future. His comrades would have been delighted with him if he hadn't fouled up everything he did with his foolish boasting.

---

21. The phrase is in the Polish edition and seems to be intended to account for a pronounced gap in continuity.

22. Benek was the code name for Baruch Weksner, who was in the first group to go into the forest and was killed there. The other man has not been identified.

23. Edwin Weiss

Recently arrived from Warsaw, Edwin had become the Warsaw faction's representative after Nusiek's death. Now he had broken off from the Warsaw faction to go into the forest. Edwin was powerfully built and had learned discipline from his years in the military. These qualities placed him high among the resistance fighters, along with his everpresent ambition, which was sometimes healthy and creative, and above all his eagerness to enter the fray. Edwin's student Adas came with him from Warsaw.[24] Adas was young, but that didn't matter. The young boys were so precocious that a year or two made no difference. What mattered most was experience, and Adas had plenty of that. He had lived through the deportations from Bydgoszcz and through the Gehenna of Warsaw. His mother had died of consumption and his father of typhus. For him there was no alternative to the forest. A man of upright character and fiery disposition, he was a natural candidate for the first unit of five.

Finally there was Ziggy.[25] Everybody knew him. Not only was he Czesiek's constant companion, but he was also his polar opposite. Although he would join Czesiek in joking and banter, Ziggy was a much more profound character. He had his own personality, and unlike Czesiek was not one for wasting words. He didn't say much, but when he did make a witty remark, there was a world of sombre wisdom in it. As everyone around him rolled on the floor in uncontrollable laughter, he would look at them as if he pitied them, as if he didn't understand what they found so funny, as if he wanted to ask, "You call this a joke, you simpletons?"

But nobody really knew him. No one understood his soul, in whose depths tragedies great and small were transpiring. Ziggy's sense of humor concealed an unusually serious outlook that constantly tormented him. The only thing they knew about Ziggy was that he was one of those manly, sensible men who could be depended on. When his mother and sister were deported, he turned inward and said nothing. Not long after, his Runka, a frail girl with a gentle soul and a beautiful soprano voice, was taken from Rymanov in a

---

24. Adas is Justyna's name for Salo Kanal.

25. Ziggy is Zygmunt Mahler, one of those killed in the first foray into the forest.

transport. Ziggy was broken. Only Dolek's warmth and heartfelt consolations managed to revive him. When he was with his movement comrades, he became more serene, but he still hadn't recovered his spirit. It was not until the call "To the forest!" was sounded that he became himself again. He was not just ready to go; he was champing at the bit. Only this call could have saved him. Supply officer of his unit of five, he succeeded in equipping them adequately with all but weapons, which they awaited eagerly.

One beautiful day Hela returned from Warsaw.[26] She entered the quarter smiling, looking flushed and animated. Dressed nicely and holding a new travel case in her hand, she walked with a firm step, acknowledging the admiring looks of passersby. It seemed the only thing she cared about was being admired. Anyone who observed the way she flirted shamelessly on the train or who saw her crossing the station, flashing her provocative smile, would have assumed she was on her way to visit her fiancee or to go on vacation. They would have been certain that she had no concern in life other than to enhance her worldly pleasures.

[BREAK IN THE TEXT]

When not a penny was left in the till and not a slice of bread in the kitchen, Hela always managed to get what was needed, as if out of thin air. When the deportations had started in Warsaw, she felt that the responsibility for saving everyone devolved on her alone. She didn't rest until she had succeeded in rescuing everyone she possibly could from that burning city. She left and reentered the ghetto several times, knowing each time she went in that she might never get out. She became the movement's most important liaison. She was able to make her way through her neverending chain of assignments by using her articulateness and her voluptuous beauty with the confidence of a woman supremely aware of her charms. None of the casual acquaintances she met in her travels suspected that Hela was smuggling weapons — that she had two Brownings hanging under

---

26. Hela Schipper was a courageous and effective courier and smuggler of weapons. She lives in Israel.

her loose sports coat and three hand weapons and a few clips of cartridges in her new bag.

-»->-<-«-

No one had ever been greeted with the outpouring of affection that was showered on Hela. The weapons she brought marked the start of a new era. Later, as she lay on Dolek's couch to get some rest, every minute someone else would come in to greet her warmly and cast a surreptitious glance around the little room, hoping to get a glimpse of the small bit of contraband which at that moment was more valuable than anything else in the world. Mira came first, then Anna, then Justyna, but none dared open the precious bag hanging on the wall.[27]

Not until Marek arrived did the door close and the inspection begin. It is impossible to describe the ecstasy inspired by those weapons. Up to this point those gathered had committed many offenses, any one of which qualified them for the gallows. But the possession of weapons was the gravest of transgressions for the population at large, and since the entire population was living under a reign of terror, it was truly a miracle that they had managed to acquire this contraband. When the invading army had conquered the country three years earlier, its first act had been to confiscate all weapons. After that, there had been meticulous searches in which even buried revolvers were discovered. Every bayonet was taken. Not even a single bullet could be concealed safely.

So it was almost unbelievable that any weapons could have gone undetected. No occupation had ever encroached so completely on every aspect of private life. Never had a civilian population been so defenseless in the face of a terrorist military regime, and now, as the movement was getting underway, everyone was obsessed with finding ways to get hold of weapons. No one had really believed weapons would ever be found.

What a joy it was to have some!

-----

27. The Mira mentioned here is Miriam Liebeskind, Dolek's sister, who was murdered in Radom in January 1943.

[BREAK IN THE TEXT]

They could even locate weapons buried in the ground. It felt marvellous to have weapons, knowing they could be used against the enemy at the appropriate time. . . .

→►◄←

Marek is busy breaking down the Browning, happy as a child just given the toy he's dreamed of. It's hard to say who is happier, a man who has finally gotten his hands on a tool of destruction or a boy who's found a new plaything. At any rate, Marek is far happier now. When he meets Dolek, the mood gets even livelier: it's as if their boyish imaginations have been rekindled. They start fantasizing about combat situations. The two of them will jump six men and disarm them. They'll round up six weapons with a single blow, enabling them to equip six more comrades. This system will guarantee a steady flow of weapons, so that in no time they can equip a whole division. It was enough to have purchased the first five weapons; the rest will be taken as spoils of war.

They were grown men. They saw life as it was and were not unaware of the pitfalls that fate might have in store. Usually when Marek got carried away by his youthful enthusiasm like a frisky colt, thirty-year-old Dolek would know how to rein him in. But now the two of them had succumbed to fantasy and were preparing to conquer the world. Actually, it wasn't just daydreaming. Everything they said was possible; the question was whether those possibilities could be realized, for they were all poised on the edge of an abyss at every moment, and an infinite number of unforeseeable circumstances could nudge them into it. And they were mere novices, facing the best-equipped and most thoroughly trained soldiers in the world.

Or could it be that they had forgotten momentarily how formidable a foe they were facing? So strong was their inner drive that they really believed they could not fail. They were fully convinced that those five weapons would make further acquisitions of weapons possible and that they would become an irresistible force, galvanizing the masses and sweeping them into the struggle. Plans had already been laid for the first unit of five to go into the forest that autumn. By spring, the forests would be swarming with multitudes of armed youths. Every fighter who fell in battle would be replaced by scores of freshly armed men. All of this they truly believed.

But things might not turn out that way. The tragic defeat in Warsaw remained fresh in our memories.[28]

-->--<--

The underground fighters in Warsaw had been set to make their move, but they suffered a severe blow the very day they were to leave for the forest. They had accumulated an arsenal and prepared a trained cadre. Of the twenty fighters who had set out for Lubielsk, some were apprehended on the train, while the rest made it safely to Miedzyrzecz. But because the conditions were not yet suitable for battle, they were forced to put off their planned action for a few days. Then came an unexpected deportation order. A few of them barely managed to escape. The rest had to be sacrificed, among them the cream of the youth. Yet there was still a strong contingent in Warsaw, including many who could replace those who had fallen. Then their leader suddenly fell into the hands of the authorities. At that point they realized the area had to be cleared of weapons and started to transfer them elsewhere. But one misfortune led to another. People were caught and weapons confiscated, even though no one had panicked and all acted with appropriate caution. Unfortunately, they were trapped. Shmuel fought to the very end to no avail. They had all conducted themselves with valor, but those who had been the soul of the uprising were wiped out. About seventy were left, but what could they accomplish without leaders or a sense of direction?

-->--<--

What had happened in Warsaw could just as easily happen in Kra-

---

28. Draenger may be referring to the January 1943 resistance. For details, see Gutman 1994, 177–200.

kow. Disaster could strike before they had even begun. In the meantime, they were already anticipating that spring would be a season of victory and freedom.

At the end of the week, the first group of fighters left for the forest.

[BREAK IN THE TEXT]

While the oldtimers in the movement were busy planning and performing acts of resistance, younger people were maturing and getting ready to join their ranks. When the decision to take up arms was reached in July, the leaders hadn't tried to persuade anyone to join them. Not wanting to lead others to their death, they agreed that only those with a burning desire to fight should do so. They believed that everyone had a right to try to save themselves.

No one knew how long the Jews could survive, but most people still felt that survival was more or less possible. Someone with private means who didn't care to look beyond his own nose, for instance, might be able to put on some sort of disguise and hole up in a remote village. Or one could possibly find a place as a laborer in a military camp and wait out the war there.

There were always opportunities to save your own skin and people who would choose self-preservation over resistance. Every individual had the right to run his own life, even if he didn't know what he was doing. In Kopaliny no one had said anything about the impending battle. Antek, Marek, and Justyna had long since given up selfish goals, and the others had no idea of how desperate their situation was.

But once Antek had said to Justyna, "You know, given what's happening to us, there's only one way to preserve your sanity. You've got to believe in the existence of a higher form of justice that will avenge us some day. You've got to believe in a world to come where we will be rewarded for our sufferings."

With an ironic smile, Justyna answered, "Can't you imagine any other way out?"

"There is another way. But that would be madness."

"Is there anything left for us but madness?"

"I haven't given the question any thought."

"How could you not think about it?" Justyna lost all self-control.

"History will never forgive us for not having thought about it. What normal, thinking person would suffer all this in silence? Future generations will want to know what overwhelming motive could have restrained us from acting heroically. If we don't act now, history will condemn us forever. Whatever we do we're doomed, but we can still save our souls. The least we can do now is leave a legacy of human dignity that will be honored by someone, some day."

They never discussed the subject again. It may well be that people were brooding over their destinies, but no one spoke of it. We were all waiting. Everyone in Krakow sensed the importance of the impending events, and everyone was eager to participate.

The fighters were pathetically young, the youngest of all being Czarna.[29] She was only fifteen, but no one would have believed it. She was a well-developed, full-figured, powerfully built girl, a genuine beauty with a crown of thick hair. Within that healthy body dwelled a strong, courageous soul. Despite her youth, she was so mature that even her elders looked to her for support. And no wonder, for she had metamorphosed into adulthood without passing through the normal stages of childhood and adolescence. One night she went to bed a child, and the next morning she woke as a woman. Twelve years old when the war broke out, Czarna was Marek's only sister, and when he was sent to prison she had cried like a baby.[30] But her grief did not prevent her from taking care of him as if she were his mother. In her fit of crying she had shed all her baby tears, and she emerged a woman who would fight not only to save a brother but also to advance a just cause. She visited him in prison every day, bringing him whatever she could get her hands on. When he was taken to a camp, she comforted their parents and kept their spirits up, never losing faith that Marek would return. When he did return, he encountered not a little sister but an equal and a friend. At that time she was not yet fourteen. Her sudden metamorphosis had fused a fresh, hardy, brave soul with a blossoming, girlish beauty. What

---

29. Czesia Draenger, Szymek's sister, a bright and precocious girl, murdered on March 19, 1943.

30. Szymek Draenger had been arrested for anti-German activities in 1939 and spent a year in the Opatów concentration camp. Then, as in 1943, Gusta turned herself in to be with him.

was most curious was that there was no trace of vanity or arrogance in her, as if it were the most natural thing in the world that yesterday she had been a child and today she had heaped onto her shoulders responsibility for the whole household. She had not even finished school.

To ensure that Czarna's education would continue in spite of the occupation, Marek and Justyna gave her lessons in the basic subjects, which her young mind soaked up like a sponge. Czarna made rapid progress in her studies, but in the first year of the war Justyna put her to work for the cause. Since Justyna didn't want to influence Czarna's ideological development unduly or to allow familial affection to interfere with the natural unfolding of the girl's youthful soul, she decided to entrust Mira with the task of continuing Czarna's education. From this point on Czarna's education proceeded along relatively conventional lines. Though she lived among people two to three years older, Czarna had no trouble keeping up with them. She outdid her companions in almost everything, but since no one called attention to her achievements, they soon forgot how precocious she was and that she had been forced into adulthood before her time. It was a pity that she would never experience childhood. Czarna's comrades didn't hesitate to involve her in all sorts of difficult assignments. She was always the youngest on a job, but she never failed to perform on the same level as the adults. She displayed the same mature competence in Krakow as she had in Kopaliny. Marek himself often called on her to perform tasks he would not entrust to some of the older people. And when he didn't call on Czarna for a particularly tough job, he would entrust it to Poldek.[31]

No one knew how long Czarna and Poldek had been friends, nor could anyone figure out how a girl so young could be capable of such intense feelings. She was as decisive and determined in her relationship with Poldek as she was in her work for the cause. Though she was young, she knew enough not to let anyone or anything come between them.

→>-<-

31. Yehuda Maimon, who lives in Israel

The first unit of five to enter the forest experienced great hardships. They were true pioneers, though you would think that since organized partisan groups were already operating in the forests, all the first unit would have had to do was to show up armed and ready, then settle down to fight—that they would only have to find the right spot, and before they knew it they would be an integral part of the organized struggle.

Our group was given a specific destination in the forest. At that time, the movement was cooperating with the Worker's Party. So with the party's commission in hand, they were to meet a guide at the railroad station.[32] The guide, who was indeed waiting, led them through the town and provided them with a night's lodging in a hut at the edge of the forest.

Our people were all fired up. It was as if they were inspired by a sacred zeal that would not permit them to think of anything but the impending action. Tomorrow they would embark on a wondrous new life. They were the first. They felt that they were blazing a trail for the whole movement, and that to prove themselves worthy of the leaders' confidence, they would have to do whatever it took to carry out their mission successfully. They looked forward to the coming action with an intense consciousness of the responsibility placed on them.

At daybreak a new guide appeared. He led them out of the hut and through the forest, but didn't seem to know the way very well and kept going around in circles. Finally he ran off, abandoning them. They hadn't a clue what to do next. It was a terrible feeling to have weapons, to be burning for action, and yet to have to stand around silently, doing nothing, not even knowing where to find the enemy. They clenched their fists in a powerless rage. Unwilling to accept the possibility that the guide had misled them deliberately, they kept circling in the forest. They wanted to believe that he had set them on the right path and that there was a partisan base somewhere in the vicinity.

They continued to circle through the forest looking for Polish

---

32. The Polish Workers Party (PPR), "established in January 1942, stressed the idea of immediate struggle" (Krakowski, 1984, 5).

partisans, but to no avail. After spending the entire day in this futile search, they eventually returned to the hut at the edge of the forest, where they were greeted coldly. The shelter had been allotted to them only for the previous night. This evening they had to break in. Once inside, they were so tired, disenchanted, and bitter that all they wanted to do was to get some rest and forget what had happened.

They took off their duffel bags and prepared for sleep. The next day, after they had rested and calmed down, they would come up with their own plan. Now they just wanted some peace and quiet. The village fell silent, and they figured that everyone in the town was asleep. Suddenly they heard a dog barking. The barking kept getting closer and closer, louder and louder. Ziggy jumped up. The boys listened attentively. Someone was approaching. Looking out the window, they saw a detachment of gendarmes coming. So, they had been betrayed! There wasn't a moment to waste. They had only a few seconds to pull themselves together, figure out what was going on, and prepare to act.

They went into action as a single person. It was a matter of life and death, and they couldn't permit themselves to die yet. There was no use trying to fight it out, since it was the five of them against a whole detachment of gendarmes. They had no choice but to make a strategic retreat. The footsteps kept coming closer and closer.

By the time the detachment reached the hut, the youths were in the forest. Surrounded by darkness and unbroken silence, they hid in the underbrush. They had dodged a bullet, but they were not yet out of danger. The police stayed on their trail, so they had to move with extreme caution. They remained in the forest for three days and three nights. Cut off from contact with the outside world and unable to get any aid, they soon ran out of food. They had only one piece of bread, which might just as well have been a symbol, since they guarded it as if it were a treasure. To quench their thirst, they drank the dew from the grass. The forest was surrounded by gendarmes. From time to time they could hear shooting, but not a single gendarme had the guts to enter the forest. The gendarmes were deathly afraid of the partisans. As soon as a single partisan was spotted, panic would spread through all the police stations in the district. Rumors were circulating that the partisans were terrorizing whole villages, that armed bands were forcing peasants to comply with their demands, that they were spreading fear and dread among the local populace, and that nobody could stop them. All those soldiers from the mightiest army of the world cowered in dread of those armed youngsters. It wasn't that the soldiers lacked self-confidence, but they preferred not to encounter unknown rebels whose exploits were being woven into colorful legends by the peasantry. To put it bluntly, the Germans were intimidated by the growing notoriety of the partisans. This was a moral victory for the underground fighters: they had deflated the pride of the conquerors and aroused fear in those who had been supremely arrogant.

When our unit of five had been seen in the village, the news spread like wildfire that a division of three hundred armed partisans was operating in the forest. It is hard to say just how the rumor got started. It seemed to have come out of nowhere. The people in the area lived in constant fear, and it was this fear that led them to betray our boys. The peasants didn't want any terrorist activities in their backyard and couldn't denounce our fighters fast enough. For two days the area around the forest was swarming with gendarmes hunting our boys, but none dared venture into the depths of the forest. They fired in at random, as if taking target practice. The noise of shooting went on without a pause until the gendarmes finally tired of the work. When they'd had enough, they declared the enemy defeated and gave up the hunt.

When they emerged after three days holed up in the forest, the fighters were tired, hungry, and exhilarated. They felt as if they had won a victory by holding out against a superior force.

But once they left the forest, they didn't know what to do. They had no roof over their heads and couldn't let themselves be seen in the village. As for the guide, he never reappeared, leaving them completely on their own. Since only the leadership could decide what to do, they had to find some way to inform the administration in Krakow what had happened. They had to find a messenger who could somehow get through to headquarters.

But they decided to take another crack at hooking up with the partisans before sending the message. They couldn't stand the thought of reporting that they had failed; it would have been too humiliating.

Though tired and hungry, they planned to continue their work that evening.

→>-<←

The autumn night was so dark that they were able to crawl right up to the police station without being noticed. When they got within earshot, they didn't hear any voices from inside. Their plan had been to take those inside by surprise, to jump and disarm them. Having overcome the enemy, they would then send a triumphant message to Krakow. The whole affair would take no more than a minute and would redeem their honor.

But those inside were on constant alert. Not for a moment did they forget that they were surrounded by a forest, and that in the forest lay young activists who were prepared to do whatever they had to. Sitting inside the well-secured police station with a heavy lock on every door, the gendarmes were not about to open the door for anyone.

So was this a defeat? Never! It was a victory. The police had showed once again how cowardly they were. They had not defeated the five fighters; they had merely hidden behind their fortifications, lacking the courage to face them.

Of course it was embarrassing for our boys to leave, repelled by nothing more than a bolted door. They could have tried to take the station by force, to blow the door out, then rush inside and grab the weapons. But they were only five and had no idea how many waited inside.

The partisan's effectiveness depends not so much on sheer strength as on the element of surprise. The partisan tries to overwhelm the enemy not with superior weapons but with his ability to keep the enemy off balance. Imagine the astonishment of a soldier armed with a heavy rifle and a bayonet who is suddenly confronted by a steely-eyed young lad with a revolver in his hand. By the time the stunned soldier has had time to figure out what the child is after, a shot has been fired. The partisan must use surprise; he has to take advantage of the optimal moment. His greatest strength lies in psychological domination. He doesn't even dream of attaining military superiority.

The minute he tries to achieve victory by means of arms alone, he ceases to be a partisan and becomes a conventional soldier.

The youths understood that. They had no false pride and were not immature, reckless daredevils. They would rather walk away from the locked door than risk their lives unnecessarily. It is important to keep your dignity even in defeat. They hadn't really been vanquished, for they hadn't lost sight of their spiritual values. Those who had bolted the doors were the cowards. Clearly they had been psychologically intimidated.

That same evening, Edwin left for Krakow. There was nothing more to be done here. They had no names or addresses, not a single experienced partisan to hook up with, no objective to take up.

They had taken every reasonable opportunity to get into the action, but everything had gone against them. The terrain had been unsuitable. The guide had betrayed them. Instead of taking them to the prearranged meeting place in the forest, he had lured them into a trap. They might all just as well have returned to Krakow, but since that could have been considered desertion, they decided to remain in the forest and await Edwin's return. In the meantime they built hiding places and scouted the area in hopes of turning up some action, but without success.

→>-<+-

The leaders locked themselves into Eva's little room, covered the glass door, and conversed in whispers.[33] Edwin lay on the couch while Dolek, Marek, Romek, and Maniek formed a semicircle around him. Edwin was telling them everything that had happened, in minute detail. They listened with increasing tension and a growing sense of anger. When the door opened a crack and Justyna's face peeped in from behind the curtain, they dismissed her with an impatient wave of the hand, signalling her not to disturb them at this critical moment.

---

33. Eva is Eva Liebeskind (Wushka), Dolek's wife, deported to Birkenau on January 19, 1943.

She withdrew obediently, though she longed passionately to be in that room with them! Since she already knew so much about what was going on, she had a right to be there among the four when the fate of their people was being weighed in the balance. But it didn't have to be Justyna — it could just as well have been Anna or Mira or Eva, any one of them, as long as at least one woman was present. Justyna was terribly worried about the five boys who had been dispatched to the forest, either to win honor or to be shamed. She had long ago come to terms with the thought that the time would come when not one of those beloved boys would be around any more. But at least let them die feeling joy and a sense of accomplishment and not just perish in the wilderness in hopelessness and despair.

Inside the room, only the men engaged in making the decision, and they didn't like the idea of withdrawal. As far as they were concerned, every withdrawal was a defeat.

→>–<←

Justyna paces irritably in front of the house, impatiently waiting for their decision. "Why worry, Justyna?" a calm inner voice whispers to her. "Have you forgotten that Dolek is inside, Dolek who holds human life sacred? He who has revealed on so many occasions that the lives of the people who have been hanged are even dearer to him than they were to those executed? How many times has he intervened to prevent the hotheads from carrying out some rash deed, just out of his love for them? As the eldest, he has felt all along that he has to keep them from letting youthful enthusiasm spur them on imprudently. He has always been like a caring rider, pulling in the reins to curb his raging beast. How often does his most fiery charge rear up and strain to go its own way? But a vigilant rider knows how to hold the beast in check. Sometimes it has been like this between Dolek and Marek. In the bloom of youth, Marek would let himself get carried away, and Dolek would have to rein him in until Marek had composed himself and slowed to the pace set by his vigilant rider.

"But by this time, Marek too can be trusted with the lives of the young men. In spite of his youth, he has learned to distinguish be-

Gusta Davidson Draenger ("Justyna"), author of the *Narrative*. All photographs reproduced by permission of Beit Lohamei Haghetaot (Ghetto Fighters House), Kibbutz Lohamei Haghetaot, Israel. Code names used in the *Narrative* appear in parentheses and quotations following given names (and nicknames, in some cases).

Gusta Davidson Draenger and
Shimson Draenger, wife and husband,
date unknown.

Shimson (Szymek) Draenger ("Marek"),
one of Akiba's leaders.

Leading members of Akiba, 1941.

Czesia Draenger ("Czarna"), Szymek's sister, a valuable movement worker who was killed March 19, 1943.

Aharon Liebeskind ("Dolek"), one of Aikiba's leaders.

Eva (Wushka) Liebeskind, movement worker and wife of Aharon Liebeskind. A cellmate of Gusta's, Wushka was deported to Birkenau on January 19, 1943.

Miriam Liebeskind ("Mira"), Aharon's sister, killed in Radom in January 1943, and Baruch Weksner ("Benek"), who was killed in the forest.

Hela Rufeisen-Schipper, a courageous and effective courier and smuggler of weapons.

Hela Rufeisen-Schipper and Szoszana Langer, 1943, Warsaw.

Gola Mira, poet, Communist, and cellmate of Gusta's.

Abraham (Laban) Leibowicz ("Romek"), one of Akiba's leaders.

Heshek Bauminger, an effective fighter and a member of the Communist-Zionist youth group Hashomer Hatzair and the PPR (Polish Worker's Party).

Maniek Eisenstein, Akiba's youngest leader, killed March 20, 1943.

Ziggi Mahler, member of Akiba. Born June 6, 1920; killed March 20, 1943.

Maimon Wasserman ("Poldek"), now Yehuda Maimon, was a courier for Akiba. He lives in Israel.

Szymon Lustgarten ("Simek"), an important movement operative.

Milek Gottlieb ("Emil"), who went to the forest to help establish a base for resistance and died there.

Juda Tennenbaum ("Czesiek"), an important movement operative.

Jadzia Strykowska (now Judy Lachman), age 12, 1938. Active in spiritual resistance, she was the leader of Pluton Laor-Dror.

Movement worker Halina Rubinek, Dolek's courier, killed March 19, 1943. Drawing by Robert Sutz from 1942 photograph. Reproduced by permission.

Movement worker Towa Fuchs ("Toska"). Drawing by Robert Sutz from 1942 photograph.

Nathan Parizer ("Nolek") helped keep 13 Jozefinska stocked with supplies.

Edwin Weiss, a student of Szymek's, one of the first group of five to go into the forest.

Ghetto walls in Krakow.

The Cyganeria Cafe, Krakow, was among the gathering places bombed by Akiba members on December 22, 1942.

Summer colony of Akiba, 1939.

Translator Roslyn Hirsch in front of 13 Jozefinska Street, Krakow, 1995.

tween bravery and madness. He has mastered his temper sufficiently to be able to stop in mid-course when he sees himself exceeding the dictates of common sense. He knows enough to withdraw, when the situation warrants."

Thinking these things, Justyna is overwhelmed by a warm thankfulness; neither their courage nor the consuming fire of the cause have led them to depreciate human life. They were ready to make sacrifices, even to face destruction, but they didn't want to waste lives. Each life had to be protected as if it were the most precious treasure. In that spirit and behind closed doors, they were now making their decision. The next day Edwin left on the first train, carrying their answer. The order was succinct: leave the forest, head for the nearest town, and await further orders.

--><--

The leadership was in a difficult situation. When they had decided in August to engage in armed struggle, they had known they weren't prepared for the task. They had all been leaders of activist youth organizations for many years, teachers who had worked hard to educate the masses. They knew the souls of their students, knew how to steer them through hazardous straits. They were models of struggle and self-sacrifice. Their leadership was inspiring, their work creative. What was most real to them in any human act was its spiritual character, and once

[BREAK IN THE TEXT]

They never acted like officers, and were not eager to lead their young followers into the furnace. The leaders were prepared to serve as privates to an experienced officer who could understand the needs of the moment and translate their ardor into heroic deeds. They searched for a leader with military experience because that was what they lacked.

Their need for someone with military experience eventually led them to hook up with the Worker's Party, though that decision also depended on a complicated chain of events and personalities.

The person most responsible for the decision to join forces with the PPR was undoubtedly Eva's cousin, Lydka.[34] Eva had always looked up to Lydka, an idealist who had sacrificed her life on the altar of the people. She had always lived to serve humanity in general rather than her own family or even herself. When the war broke out she was in prison, serving a fifteen-year sentence in "the fortress." She had served three years of her sentence when the war started, and it was then that she escaped with some other prisoners. Once again she plunged into the whirlwind of altruistic work. She was reunited with her husband, until the chaos of the war tore him from her. Left alone with an infant, she requested a furlough from the party and gave up her work temporarily to devote all her time to taking care of her little one. A mother in the fullest sense of the word, she loved the child more than she loved her own life. Although her commitment to the revolution in no way diminished her maternal affection, she sought eventually to leave the child with relatives in order to return to work.

One day she rushed into the house of an acquaintance, laid the baby on the bed, and went to the city. The baby was beautiful and well cared for. Although the mother herself was half-dead with hunger, you could see that she had poured the full force of her love into the baby. When she returned, the baby was no longer alive. She shook off the pain and went back to work. She lived with Eva's parents, which is how she found out about our movement. She and Dolek understood each other instantly and became fast friends. Marek also found himself under her spell. To them she was the ideal mature woman, a fierce fighter with a genuinely female heart. Influenced by her powerful personality and unselfish dedication, Dolek and Marek became less distrustful of Communist ideology and decided to establish a connection with the Worker's Party. They wanted to work hand in hand, to share everything, but participation was unequal. Some offered their youth and perhaps their lives, while others contributed only their experience. It was soon clear that there would not only be an inequality in the degree of dedication, but also in the extent of participation.

---

34. Gola Mira, a poet and a woman no less extraordinary than Gusta. Gola had been arrested as a member of the illegal Communist Party.

[BREAK IN THE TEXT]

The situation grew steadily more critical. Lydka did what she could to compensate for shortcomings and to alleviate tension between the two groups. She fretted constantly about everyone who was sent out, but that did not help things any. The fact is that Lydka had deceived them on one count: the Worker's Party had not operated in this territory until very recently. It was only after Lydka had returned to action that the party's operations had gotten started, and now it was the influx of highly motivated and enthusiastic Jewish youth who had gotten the party's activities flourishing.

During long deliberations, Lydka said, "It's true that we have little experience, but if we work with the party, we can gain experience while buying time."

The movement leaders responded: "You want to buy time at our expense, but at the price we're being asked to pay, we may as well hang on to our independence."

"Don't split off now," she cajoled, using her feminine charm. "If we remain united, we'll be strong."

"No. First we have to develop as an independent force. Then we'll come to you as equals. We won't have to depend on you, and there won't be any hierarchy."

On this note, the two groups parted.

While the leadership debated their course of action, the occupying forces continued plundering the masses. The bloodletting went on while the government exacted tributes of silver, gold, furs, and money. The Jewish youth ate dry crusts, lived in attics and cellars, walked around in boots with holes in them, owned no more than the shirts on their backs, and managed to raise money for their conspiratorial activities only with the greatest difficulty. Was there any point in procrastinating? They would do what they had to. Anything they could do to achieve their aims was not only justified but a matter of historical necessity.

They started operating independently, which meant taking on more projects and more responsibility. They began to feel better about what they were doing. The fact that they didn't have to depend on anyone else gave them enormous satisfaction. They entered this new phase full of courage and resolve.

The first step was to reorganize their fiscal affairs. For a long time their finances had needed restructuring. It appeared that their budget would run to thousands of *zloty* a week. The membership of the movement had increased substantially, and though the amount required to maintain a single fighter was trifling, the total was starting to add up. Then there were administrative and travel expenses to be considered, and above all the cost of purchasing weapons, which ran into thousands upon thousands. The books showed a chronic deficit.

Romek was the treasurer. How he managed to raise money remained a mystery. Someone would mention that money was needed immediately to cover an essential expense, whereupon Romek would disappear, only to turn up a short time later with a portfolio bulging with cash, thus saving the day. When the first audit of the books was conducted, it turned out that the treasury owed Romek 11,000 zloty. While the technical bureau did bring in a substantial income, even that wasn't enough.[35] More money had to be raised, and not necessarily by conventional means. The time had come to abandon old-fashioned scruples. After all, the authorities had no qualms about confiscating the hard-earned money of Jews who'd been brutally murdered.

After the aborted venture into the forest, three new missions were undertaken simultaneously. One was set up to meet the movement's urgent need for money. This assignment went to a five-man unit reinforced with two additional fighters: Harry from Maniek's group and Ignace from Romek's group.[36] Harry was a broad-shouldered, cautious, unselfish man, while Ignace was young, agile, and bitter. The unit was equipped with weapons and appropriate documents, then split into two smaller groups. One, a threesome, was made up of Edwin, Emil, and Harry, who were not only big and physically imposing, but also cultured and multilingual. Any money they man-

---

35. The technical bureau brought in funds by selling identification cards and other forged documents. For further information on income sources, see Rotem 1994, where a ghetto fighter describes instances in which he "confiscated" funds for the underground.

36. Harry is Chaim Sternlicht and Ignace, Judah Szmerlowicz.

aged to get their hands on was to be turned over to the Krakow administration.

The remaining four — Benek, Ziggy, Ignace, and Adas — were ordered to explore the forest, scout the surrounding area thoroughly, and get to know the terrain and the neighborhood intimately; in short, their mission was to prepare the way for the movement to start operating in the forest on its own.

A third group was given the job of setting up a network of private dwellings around the forest, each of which was to be furnished so it could be inhabited by a movement operative. The plan was for the fighters to leave the forest after each sortie and lie low for a week or two, either in the city or in one of the furnished dwellings. This third mission was assigned to Eva, Klara, and Hela, who left immediately to seek out appropriate living quarters. The movement was positioning itself to act as a self-sustaining entity.

—➤—◄—

We felt like people in a burning building, not yet completely enveloped in flames. Since there was no way to exit the building or extinguish the fire, we did not doubt that the flames would soon consume us all. Yet all we could do was watch the conflagration and wait for it to reach us. But some outlying branches of the movement had not yet been affected by the deportations, and we wanted to warn them about the impending aktzias, so the fighters would not be taken by surprise. One town still untouched by the deportations was Tomaszow, where Mirka had labored long and devotedly to train a generation of workers for the movement. She believed that our only hope lay in this younger generation.

Now that the wave of deportations was drawing closer to her own nest, she took responsibility for defending it. She prepared to set off on one of her Krakow-to-Tomaszow excursions; once again she would smuggle herself out of the Krakow Ghetto and into the Tomaszow Ghetto to rejoin her comrades in arms. But this time she intended to sound the call to arms rather than to paint her usual pleasant pictures of the future.

In preparing for these hazardous trips, Mirka would betray no hint of anxiety, and she always returned exuding happiness and carrying documents and money she had collected to buy weapons. Joy beamed from her face, which never lost its blissful glow, even in anger. She approached every problem with complete calm, with an almost childlike trust.

It was so exhilarating to watch her prepare for these trips that her apartment would fill up with evening visitors. Everyone wanted to watch her bustling around, preoccupied with preparations and completely unruffled, as though she'd given no thought whatever to the unpredictable dangers in store.

Anna once told Justyna, "Mirka is probably the bravest of us all, because courage is not just a matter of being able to suppress your fear and survive while you're standing in the police station, but of not even trembling for a second, of not feeling fear at all. Mirka really doesn't know what it's like to be afraid."

Mirka was constantly at risk because it wasn't easy for her to disguise herself as a non-Jew. She was small, with quick but dignified movements. But what was most difficult to conceal were her raven tresses and her jet black eyes. Sparks leaped from those eyes, and her smile generated a friendly intimacy that seemed to enclose everyone in its embrace. If anyone looked at her suspiciously, she would disarm suspicion with her cheerful, untroubled visage. She made her way with a charisma that was hard to resist.

Soon the workers from Tomaszow started arriving in Krakow. The first to show up were Irka and Halina, who were assigned liaison duties.[37] A liaison point headed by Alek had been functioning for some time.[38] Alek stayed at his post constantly, receiving people as they streamed in. Those arriving from Tomaszow went there to get their orders, which were issued from Krakow every few hours. Those who were supposed to leave were given instructions and money, while those who were staying received either a pass to the ghetto or a place in the city where they could spend the night. In that way scores of people passed through Alek's office, and more

---

37. Halina is Halina Rubinek, Dolek's nineteen-year-old courier, who was murdered on March 19, 1943.

38. Alek is Alexander Goldberg, murdered on April 29, 1943, trying to escape from Montelupich prison. The liaison point was at 26 Wielopole Street.

people kept coming in a steady flow. New recruits eager to fight showed up continually, and the network of dwellings kept expanding. When Irka got to Krakow, she was immediately dispatched to the outpost in Denbitzy. New groups of five were being set up continually. The only thing holding them back was the anticipated signal from the forest, which they awaited eagerly.

Finally, one Friday morning, Zygmunt and Adas showed up in Krakow. They were deathly pale as they reported to Alek, and they demanded to see Dolek and Marek, who were contacted without delay.

It was a dismal morning. The atmosphere was oppressive. Gray clouds hung over the city. The heavens should have burst into tears. The streets should have wrapped themselves in shrouds, and shrieks of despair should have reverberated through the city. All eyes should have gushed tears. Yet nothing of the sort happened. Crowds strolled through the streets. Passers by jostled and shoved each other in their haste. No one paid attention to anyone else. Mundane concerns drove them on, worries about bread, about the aimlessness of their lives, even about their own nerves. Bearing the heavy burden of life under the occupation, a weak person first sagged, then bent all the way to the ground, and finally collapsed.

The two young men walked through the crowd slowly with firm steps, gazing at the pavement, their sad foreheads lowered. As they moved forward, their hearts beat quietly. They were the bearers of distressing news. It was their painful duty to have to hurl bitter fruit into the smiling faces of their friends, to deliver a message in words dripping with blood.

Benek, Adas, Zygmunt, and Ignace had gone into the forest and isolated themselves. They had found a suitable spot and put up tents. The work had started. Day after day they had surveyed the terrain, drawn maps, become familiar with the area, explored possible launching spots for guerrilla attacks, sought out objectives, and set up bases for operations. They had devised escape routes and had thoroughly familiarized themselves with the entire region within a perimeter of fifteen miles. They had built bunkers and prepared the ground for future operations. They spent all their time in the forest, which became their world. They rarely ventured out, even to go to the village. They knew only one or two peasants who lived at the edge of the forest, and every few days one of them would steal cautiously to the edge of the forest for some food, and then return quickly.

The village was a dangerous place. The police seemed to be on constant alert. The neighborhood looked as though the entire population had left. The roads were empty. A deafening silence reigned day and night. Not even the peasants enjoyed freedom of movement, and any stranger was immediately looked upon with suspicion. Everyone was afraid of the partisans, so a stranger was suspected of being either an insurgent or an enemy spy who had parachuted into the region undetected. Documents were no help in proving a stranger's innocence. The only verdict was guilty. The boys were not particularly attracted to the village and were content to stay in the forest. They didn't miss other people or the bustle of the city. They were too intent on their work to be bored.

One Tuesday, their supplies having run out, they were forced to look for supplies in the village. Benek and Ignace left camp at dusk and emerged from the forest in thick darkness. Through the dark mist of that autumn evening, they noticed a small hut. They stole into it and sat down at the table. The room was dimly lit by a smoky lamp next to the wall. A cricket was chirping somewhere. They didn't utter a word.

Suddenly there was a loud knock on the door. A gendarme was standing in the doorway, and behind him a policeman. In the hall stood a third figure, barely visible. That third person was none other than the forest ranger, with a carbine hanging from his shoulder. Three of them against two of us. Apparently the darkness had not concealed the boys adequately, and someone had run into the village to denounce them. The three officials stood lined up, carbines in hand, ready for a scuffle.

The boys didn't move a muscle. They sat with their hands in their pockets, looking at the intruders indifferently. Maybe they even feigned surprise, as if they could see no connection between their presence in this place and the appearance of the armed men. They calculated the possibilities. The superiority of the other side was undeniable. To attack would be madness. There could be no question of engaging in an open fight. They had to wait for an opportune moment. They waited in resounding silence, each side measuring the other with their eyes. The lamp near the wall kept on flickering.

"Get up!" shouted the gendarme. "Documents!"

They reached into their pockets slowly and laid the papers on the table, nonchalant. They were in no hurry. A thick paw grabbed the papers.

"Do you have any weapons?"

"We don't!"

"We'll soon see about that!"

"Yes, we'll see," murmured Benek.

A pair of wild eyes glared at him savagely.

"Off with your clothes," he shouted.

Benek bent over, three guns hovering above his head. He pretended not to see them. He moved slowly. First he would take off his boots. Which one first? Maybe the right. It does not come off easily. Something is stuck. He pulls harder. There it goes! He pulls out a gun and rises urgently. A shot rings out. His aim is accurate. The gendarme's huge body sags slowly to the floor, blood gushing everywhere. The other two stand motionless, paralyzed by astonishment. Their frozen hands are glued to their carbines. Another shot rings out, this time less accurate. It hits the policeman in the right shoulder. He rolls to the wall, then faints. At that point the third one rouses himself out of his stupor and aims his weapon at Benek.

This is the critical moment. Ignace, who was unarmed, was standing off to the side. The group of four had only two guns; Benek and Ignace had taken one to the village, and the other was with Adas and Zygmunt. Ignace stood there helpless, clenching his fists, biting his lips. He looked on, saw everything, but couldn't do anything. This was the most difficult moment of his life.

One more second and a shot would be fired from the carbine, straight into Benek's temple. If Ignace had only had a weapon, he could have taken out the third thug and they would have been home free. He would have had a clear shot. But his clenched fists were empty. It was only his eyes that penetrated the forest ranger. In agony, his entire soul concentrated itself into his dark pupils. He was breathing heavily. Benek's life was hanging by a thread. Right now, at this very moment, the most terrible thing was about to happen.

Though it seemed like ages, it was only a fraction of a second, a blink of an eye. A shot was fired. Benek swayed and fell. The crash of the falling body brought Ignace to his senses. Now it was his turn. He stood up proudly, prepared to die.

In the forest, Adas and Ziggy waited all evening for their comrades to return. Every few minutes they left their hiding place and listened. Midnight came and passed. It was a dark night; perhaps they were lost. Ziggy went to look for them. He came back despondent.

"We have no choice," he said. "We must wait till morning."

They forgot their hunger and fatigue. They couldn't sleep. Their anxiety mounted with each moment. The fire burned out, and the cold penetrated them. By dawn they were exhausted and at the limits of their endurance.

Something must have happened in the village, but they forced themselves to be calm and wait at least until noon. The hours dragged on. Finally, when the sun reached its zenith, they stole silently to the edge of the forest. They proceeded as unobtrusively as possible. They didn't see a living soul. It seemed as if everyone in the village had died. Then they saw a peasant in the distance. Recognizing him, they cautiously left the thicket.

The peasant also saw them. He blinked his eyes stealthily and covered his lips with his finger, signalling them to be cautious.

"Don't go to the village, gentlemen."

"Why not?"

"They're sniffing around like dogs today."

"Why? Has something unusual happened?"

"Yes. Yesterday, in my hut," he said, lowering his voice, "they shot two brave young men."

They looked at each other.

"Did you know them?"

"They sometimes used to come to me."

"What were their names?"

"Ah, how should I know?" he answered, waving his hands.

"What did they look like?"

He described them perfectly. There was nothing more to consider. Benek and Ignace were no longer alive.

"They died like men," the peasant concluded. "Real brave men. Probably ours," he whispered.

He became pensive. "You'd better not go into the village," he warned again. "It would be a pity, gentlemen. . . ." He turned on his heel and left hurriedly.

They returned to the forest, but there was nothing they could do. The two of them would not be able to accomplish anything by themselves. They would have to inform the leadership. They had to do something to relieve their pain, to tell what had happened to someone they could trust. They waited in the forest for a few more hours. In the evening they sneaked out to the station. By Friday morning, they were in Krakow.

They didn't collapse; they didn't give in to despair; they didn't even shed a tear. That was how it had to be. Their comrades had died like heroes. They had kept their composure to the very end and conducted themselves like genuine soldiers. The two shots Benek fired were calculated. No one could have acted more decisively. The only reason their mission was not a complete success was that Ignace did not have a weapon. Otherwise, that unyielding lad would have finished the job. It would have taken only one more shot, and Ignace wouldn't have missed. Then they could have disappeared into the darkness of the forest with the three captured carbines. By the time the authorities mounted a full-scale search, the fighters would have been long gone. Everything hinged on that one missing shot. The moral to be drawn from this incident was clear: anyone going into the field must be armed. Two people had to be sacrificed for that priceless lesson.

That was the movement's first step on a road from which it never retreated. The two victims became, as it were, the cornerstones of a magnificent structure. Once you start to build, you've got to finish. Whoever has sacrificed two courageous victims must press the battle further to redeem their brave acts.

True, the inner pain was excruciating. Yet you had to learn to suppress sorrow; you had to find the inner strength to bounce back from a tragic loss. You had to become tough. You had to learn to cozy up to the angel of death, who would surely be visiting the fighters with ever greater frequency from now on.

This was their answer.

⇥⇤

Once again they were seated on the couch in Eva's small room, behind locked doors. They didn't lower their heads or wring their hands, but conducted their conference with profound serenity. The words Dolek had just spoken were still ringing in the air when Justyna entered the room. They greeted her in silence, looking at her and returning to their own thoughts. She sat quietly on the edge of the sofa.

She didn't even dare to breathe. Huddled together in that small room, the four of them seemed to project a majestic aura. A small lamp on the night table cast a dim light on their faces. Shadows flickered on the pallid wall, where their profiles were cast in sharp lines. They sat motionless, as if turned to stone. They looked as if the very worst had already happened to them. Whatever came next they would take without flinching and without regret. Justyna greedily absorbed the deep calm. She had not heard the words Dolek had uttered just before she entered, but looking at those hard shadows etched on the wall, she knew everything. The deep calm penetrated her slowly.

Marek gave a sudden start and looked up. It was only then that he noticed his wife.

"Justyna," he whispered, "go upstairs to Hela. She is waiting at Genia's to hear the results of the meeting.[39] Tell her she leaves tonight. Tell her to get ready for the trip. She'll be returning to Rzeszow, where she's to wait for Edwin, Emil, and Harry, or for word from them.[40] Tell her to be brave."

"All right," she said, and got up to leave.

"One minute!" He stopped her. "Tell her to report here before she leaves the quarter. I'll give her money and instructions. Mietek is also leaving today. He's off to Lvov, not Rzeszow, but if they want they can travel together."

Since Genia lived in the same building, Justyna ran up to the third floor, where she found Genia and Hela together. They sat at the table, engaged in conversation. Hela had a fair complexion and full,

---

39. Genia is Genia Wortsman, deported to Auschwitz on January 19, 1943, where she died.

40. Harry is Samuel Gottlieb, commander of the first fighting unit, who was killed in the forest.

rosy cheeks. Genia was pale, with beautiful, smooth hair. Her lovely eyes were staring intently at Hela, taking in every word. She still didn't know what had happened. For the time being, no one was supposed to know. Justyna leaned over to Hela and kissed her affectionately. Hela hugged her and pressed her close.

"So, she's suffering," Justyna thought. "You would never know it from the lively way she's telling stories to Genia. This girl knows how to control herself." Justyna felt respect for Hela and looked into her eyes. Hela stared back with a sad gaze, to which Justyna responded with a meaningful smile. As Justyna pulled up a chair, Genia left the room.

They conversed in hushed tones, unburdening themselves of their deepest feelings. Each found new strength in the other. The next day everything was back in order. Hela was at her station in Rzeszow, and Mietek in Lvov.

After Marek had returned from Lvov, they had started to send out [text missing]. Possibilities had opened up for crossing the border into Hungary. But this was a separate matter, unrelated to the work of the partisans. Deep inside they still believed they would survive. Although each of them was ready to die in battle, they couldn't endure the thought that they might all be destroyed. They could not bear to think that the war would end, an armistice would be signed, and not a single one of them would be alive. They were troubled by the chance that nobody would survive to bear witness.

If even a small number were saved, they would become a living monument to the movement. In Palestine, the movement was a viable entity, but those in Palestine would never know how those here fought and died.

Some wanted Marek and Romek to send a group of people across the green border, those who were typically Jewish in appearance and who were therefore of limited use in this kind of work. If such a group should survive the war, its members would not only carry out their mission of bearing witness, but would also perpetuate the spiritual values of the movement. At present, however, none of them was willing to leave his or her comrades for anything. They were of one mind, and their lives were dedicated to the struggle. Still, the feeling lingered that a small group should be prepared to make the trip.

Dolek was against it. He laid the situation out in the starkest terms: "Either we resist or we try to save ourselves. If we resist, then everyone must fight. Anyone who doesn't is a deserter!"

—➤—◄—

Though no consensus was reached, it was still possible that they would decide to save a remnant of their people. If they did, those to be saved would have to be ready to set out immediately.

A voice at another movement center was addressing the same problem.

Jozek was in Kielce, where he and Antek had organized a youth group. Communication between Kielce and Krakow occurred with great frequency, and Justyna was especially active in maintaining the connection. It was at about this time that Jozek informed us that he had recruited his close friend Wladyslaw.[41] They had been drawn to each other by their common interests in literature and culture. Jozek wrote literary criticism, while Wladyslaw was interested in drama and wrote plays. They had been part of a clique of young artists who never strayed outside their circle and who had never volunteered to do any community work. They were elevated souls who could subdue the celestial spheres with their ideas but were as helpless as children when it came to functioning in the real world. It was not until the work at Kopaliny attracted Jozek that his youthful energy began to show itself, and he soon developed a great dedication to the movement.

Justyna went to Kielce to talk to Jozek and Wladyslaw about their projects. When she arrived, Jozek began to speak.

"We're far away from Krakow, and because we're not at the center of the action, we see certain things in a different light. You focus on the activities of the partisans, but here we have other issues demanding our attention, issues we can't afford to neglect. Consider the plight of our friends here, and I don't mean only the young literati, but the whole circle of Jewish artists, with some talents just

---

41. Wladyslaw is Israel Schreibtafel, a young playwright who wrote a play, *Rabbi Akiba,* about the Jewish Fighting Organization; he died in Mauthausen.

beginning to bloom and others in full blossom. Only a few are still with us, and even they are slowly disappearing. Those who haven't been swept away in the deportations are dying of starvation. No one knows who will survive, but — "

"I doubt anyone will," Justyna interjected.

"But just in case somebody does survive," Jozek retorted, "better that it should be one of those unique souls through whom the spirit of the whole people speaks. Do you realize that we've reached a point of creative stagnation? Many of those who have survived this long are completely bland and lack uniqueness. But there are still some extraordinary creative talents here and there, and the task of the fighting youth is to preserve that creative core and keep it from being exterminated. This is surely as noble a task as the armed struggle. What do you think?"

"Keep talking! Just go ahead and talk! Tell me how you see the situation. But I don't believe a word of it. I don't believe it's possible to save anyone."

"I believe it is possible. I'll get back to practicalities later, but first I want to discuss the abstract issue. Disregard what I said about those with a divine spark. First we must protect our families. You said we should gamble everything on one roll of the dice, that we should all go down together in a frenzied convulsion of resistance. But isn't it enough for each person to throw away his own life? Do we have to throw in our parents, spouses, and children as burnt offerings? How can we concentrate only on the work when our dearest ones face annihilation and our thoughts keep returning to their fate? Never in human history have there been revolutionaries who would throw everything onto the funeral pyre, even those dearest to them. Revolutionaries have always been willing to sacrifice themselves, but at least they felt secure about the safety of their homes and families. We must safeguard our families."

"You would have my heartfelt approval if you were to choose to save your families. And I'm sure no one in the leadership would say a word against it. Everyone would accept it with relief. After all, this lies close to all of our hearts. Just come up with a plan and do whatever it takes to implement it, and then — "

"We need people to help."

"You'll get them."

"Clever and brave."

"There's no shortage of those."

"Of course we'll also need money."

They presented a detailed plan to her. She listened attentively, though she was very tired. It was almost midnight. She forced herself to follow their thoughts. But it wasn't only fatigue that distracted her; something inside her rebelled against this new project. An inner voice told her it was mere fantasy.

"Will you convey every word of our plan to the leadership?"

"I'll do it, but I must confess that I'll be doing it without conviction. I don't believe your plan will accomplish anything. And the way I present it might work against it. I don't think I can present it in the best light, and if you want to convince someone to accept something novel, you've got to be enthusiastic. You can present this better than I can . . ."

"You're right."

"Let Wladyslaw go to Krakow, and I'll arrange for him to meet with Dolek and Marek."

"We have to act quickly, because every wasted minute could cost us dearly."

"I understand. Let's make it the day after tomorrow."

That's where they left it. Justyna returned to Krakow, but she couldn't shake off her sadness. She just couldn't stop thinking of what had happened to Benek and Ignace. And they still hadn't heard anything from the other three boys who had gone in search of the golden fleece. By now they should have given some indication that they were still alive. But so far, nothing—not a word to Hela, and no message to Krakow. Not the slightest scrap of news, though they had been gone for two weeks. Something must have happened. You could imagine a million ways the boys might find themselves trapped. No one wanted to admit the terrible thought that kept insinuating itself into their minds. Everybody waited anxiously for some small sign. Justyna couldn't stop thinking about an inescapable avalanche tumbling down on them from a summit.

Take the case of that brave, pretty girl, Anka. She had gone to Rozwadow, taken an apartment, and found a job that paid well.[42]

---

42. Anka is Anka Fischer.

Then came the blackmailer. It wasn't money he wanted, but sexual favors. She resisted bravely. But when she refused to give in, the word "Jewess" was dropped. The next thing she knew, she found herself in prison. She didn't confess to anything and denied the accusation bravely. She wanted to go on working.

Someone had even tried to intervene on her behalf. Julek went to the prison.[43] He tried to use his counterfeit Lithuanian citizenship, which was supposed to clear the way for him. Nothing worked. Her self-assured manner assuaged their suspicions a bit, but the officials still refused to release her. She couldn't go on kidding herself indefinitely. She was done for. They kept putting off sentencing her, but her case was hopeless. And that was just the beginning.

When Justyna thought about all of this, she couldn't help becoming despondent. Everyone kept talking about a beautiful, free, victorious spring, but in fact fall had barely started and the ranks were already thinning. It was twilight when Justyna reached Krakow. The city was enveloped in a thick fog. She walked slowly. She had to keep up her buoyant outer appearance, since one telltale slip could give her away, but it wasn't easy to feign lightheartedness while steeped in such sad thoughts. Sustaining that artificial smile that you had to wear at all times was torture to her, and tired her to the limits of her endurance. She heaved a sigh of relief when she finally stepped into Alek's office. She was among her own, especially since Dolek was there.

"Shall we go together?" he asked.

"With the greatest of pleasure," she answered.

She took hold of his arm, and they entered the Jewish Quarter arm in arm.

So much warmth and love was packed into that one sentence that Dolek responded instinctively by embracing her with an overflow of tenderness.

Dolek had always understood her better than anyone else. She often yearned for him, the way seamen in a storm long for a calm harbor. He had a quality that encouraged you to tell him everything, to open your heart and release your sorrows. He would listen intently without interrupting, and just by listening he would lift the

---

43. Julek is Samuel Dembus.

rock from your heart. After he'd heard you out, he would respond with clear and affectionate words that would make you feel as if you had just returned from confession[44] and cleansed your soul. He made you stronger, and you felt like a better person when you were with him. You felt that your problems had been solved and your suffering would soon pass. He inspired a brighter view of life.

"You know, Dol, I can put up with anything. The only thing I can't stand are those long trips that take me far from our people. When I find myself surrounded by a world where I don't belong, I feel so bad that I start choking. It's not as if I can't move comfortably in that world. I can adapt to it. I'm familiar with its culture. I have the right looks. They all treat me well on the outside. Yet I feel as if I'm suffocating out there."

"I can imagine what you must feel," Dolek answered. Until then he had worked exclusively in the Jewish Quarter. The Jewish environment meant more to him than anything, and he couldn't picture a future without it.

"When I think," Justyna went on, "that soon all the communities our people have built will disappear from the earth, that not a trace will remain, then I swear to God I'd rather die than live to see that day. I don't want to dig the grave our culture will be buried in. I don't want to live on the site of the ruins of our people. I don't want to . . ."

"Justyna!" he said suddenly. "There's so much anger pent up in me that sometimes — " He hesitated a moment. "Sometimes I wish I had no responsibility to anyone else. Then I wouldn't have to behave myself or worry about sparing anyone's feelings. I would just throw myself into the struggle. I would sow devastation around me until I perished, and I would die satisfied."

He slipped his hand out from under her arm and quickened his pace, breathing heavily. He projected his shoulders forward as if he were clearing the road ahead. They were crossing a bridge over the

---

44. Draenger uses "confession" in the original text. Though confession is a Catholic practice, we must remember that the members of Akiba, though strong in their Jewish identities, were also somewhat assimilated; most had received a conventional Polish education. Living in an overwhelmingly Catholic country, and having many Catholic friends, they would have been familiar with the practice of confession. Like American Jews, they understood the majority culture. Draenger says this almost outright in the next paragraph.

Vistula, and the hazy streetlights disappeared completely in the thick fog.

Justyna looked at Dolek, feeling his pain. His face was pale, and his eyes sparkled in the darkness. His jaw moved strangely. She understood the expression on his face. He always looked this way when a storm brewed inside him. This was not the tender Dolek to whom people came running when they needed someone to ease their pain. This was Dolek the fighter, who put armed struggle above all else. For this Dolek, the fight took precedence over his mother, his wife, his sister, his kin, his friends, and even over his own life, so rich with promise.

→>-<-

Justyna had set up an apartment in a beautiful villa outside the Jewish Quarter.[45] The apartment consisted of a large and pleasant room with two windows, a kitchen, and a veranda. It was furnished modestly but tastefully and glowed with domestic tranquility. There were flowers on the table, curtains on the windows, and pictures hanging here and there to give the place a homey feeling.

In this cozy nest, Justyna was to play the role of an ailing wife spending the golden autumn in the resort region of Podhale. Here little Witek would frolic untroubled in the garden. In the afternoons, he and his aunt would go out for a walk. Sometimes they rented a little boat and ventured out onto the calm waters of the Raba River. Marek returned in the evening, after a full day's work in the office. Since he used to take the bus to Krakow every day, it was not long before the other regular bus passengers got to know him. When word began to spread that Marek worked for an important firm, passengers would step aside to give him a place, even when the bus was full. People would get out of his way because they feared him. His military bearing, his firm expression, his resolute figure created the impression that he was engaged in some sort of secret work for the government and was very well situated. He cut such an intimidating figure that no one wanted to tangle with him. There was an air of mystery about him that aroused curiosity. People gave him a

---

45. The apartment was in Rabka.

wide berth, not wanting to take any chances. Nobody suspected that he was a Jew and that every trip he took was for some subversive purpose. Nobody suspected that cozy suburban apartment of housing the movement's entire technical bureau.

A small desk and all sorts of office equipment had been assembled in one corner of the room, away from the window. Nothing was lacking, not even a typewriter. No self-respecting office need have felt any shame at being thus equipped. And yet there was nothing here to arouse suspicion. The neighbors were well aware that the master of the house was accustomed to bringing his work home from the office on some of his days off, so he could spend more time with his family and make their stay in the village more pleasant. No one saw anything suspicious in his frequent trips to the city; they assumed that the couple could afford to keep up a high standard of living. While this external image of a prosperous, comfortable household served to deflect suspicion, the business of an underground movement was being conducted inside the house.

Thus they carried on a double deception, with Witek playing a dual role. First, raised with a keen sense of the traditional Jewish spirit, he was nevertheless able to conceal it from the eyes of the world without renouncing it. Although he was only six, he already understood that he was a Jew, and he wanted desperately to remain one. But he also understood that in order to remain a Jew he would have to conceal that fact, at least for a while. His sharp young mind had already grasped the basic principle of the conspiracy. Not only was he able to hold his own tongue, but he also kept the adults from foolish indiscretions. He didn't permit them to use words with double meanings. He was more discreet than the others and retained the dignified bearing of a dutiful Jewish child. And the little one also played his part in the second conspiracy, although he did not really know what was going on. With his child's ease he radiated so much light and joy in the household that no one would have guessed what lurked under the cloak of normality. Yet he so yearned to live within his tradition that, in spite of the many diversions he could now indulge in, a deep sadness descended on his soul. Whenever his uncle was about to leave for Krakow, he would beg of him, "Don't tell grandma how we live here, because I'm ashamed of it."

Their days passed in a haze of domestic tranquility, but in the evenings real life took over. Usually Witek was asleep by the time

Marek got home, and even when he wanted to wait up to see his uncle, they would eat supper quickly and put him to bed right after. Only then would Marek tell Justyna what was going on in the movement. Justyna soaked up his stories and sorely regretted being tucked away in this quiet town while so many important things were happening. But she was needed here daily, and every minute here she was carrying out a vital task.

Following supper and Marek's report, once everything had quieted down and the lights had gone out in the village, the two of them would get to work. The windows were completely covered, the door locked and bolted. All the materials appeared on the desk, and the work proceeded rapidly. Sometimes they worked like this until two or three in the morning.[46] They had to wake up before six so Marek could make the seven o'clock bus. The work was exhausting for both of them, but more so for Marek. After his nights of little sleep, he had to set out for the city looking well rested and self-assured. He could not afford to show any signs of fatigue.

Though Hanka lived only twenty minutes away, she was supposed to keep her distance from them.[47] The two concealed bases of operation in the town were intended to be completely independent. But how could Hanusha stay home by herself in the villa when Justyna and Witek were only a few hundred steps away? I don't quite know how to describe their relationship, whether to call it friendship or sisterly love. During the long months of separation while Hanka was in Warsaw, she had yearned for Justyna whenever terror, misery, or despair had assailed her soul. At such moments, she would send her thoughts out to Justyna, as if to some far-off and peaceful realm. Now, after a separation of a year and a half, they were finally together again. They wanted to take advantage of every moment, so Hanusha would come early every morning and remain till late afternoon. The neighbors assumed that she was a nanny who helped the lady of the house with housework and caring for the child.

---

46. Their work consisted of forging documents and writing and publishing the underground newspaper *Hechalutz Halochem* (The fighting pioneer). The paper, issued every Friday, consisted of about ten typed pages. The editorial staff (chiefly Gusta and Szymek) duplicated about 250 copies of the typescript, which were distributed by pairs of fighters in Krakow and its environs.

47. Hanka Blas, shot in Bochnia, April 1943.

It was an opportunity for them to make up for lost time, an opportunity for two souls to fuse into one.

Hanusha was also Marek's courier. They had to get the work they finished each night to Krakow the next day, but it would have been reckless for Marek to carry all of it himself. So Hanusha would load her basket with eggs, mushrooms, and apples, put on a kerchief, and get on the bus, as if she were going to market. This was how she carried the material, sometimes sitting right next to Marek on the bus and pretending not to know him. At noon, when she returned to the town, Witek would often spot her coming through the forest and run to meet her. As far as Witek was concerned, Hanusha was as much a member of the family as Uncle and Justyna.

One Sunday evening, Witek and Justyna had set the table for a festive supper and were waiting impatiently for Marek and Hanusha to return. It was long past eight o'clock. At long last they heard a creaking on the porch, and Hanusha appeared in the doorway.

"Finally!" they burst out simultaneously.

"I've returned by myself."

"Why?" Fear gripped Justyna's throat.

"Don't worry. Marek had to stay behind."

Justyna breathed a sigh of relief. "Didn't he send any work for me?"

"No. But he wants you to come to Krakow tomorrow."

Justyna went pale again. Her mother was still in the quarter. It had been agonizing for Justyna to decide to leave Krakow. She had vowed many times not to leave her mother, but in the end she had been obliged to put loyalty to the movement above her concern for her elderly mother. Still, she suffered incessant pangs of guilt. Her anxiety about her dear mother, whom she worshipped, gave her no peace. Now she turned white because she had guessed everything.

"Calm down," said Hanka. "There is going to be an aktzia in Krakow. But it won't happen before Wednesday or Thursday. You'll certainly have a chance to get your mother out."[48]

Justyna did not answer.

---

48. The aktzia alluded to here refers to the deportations of October 28, 1942. According to Ainsztein, "Some 6,000 Jews were rounded up and dispatched to Belzec, while several hundred were murdered on the spot" (1974, 826).

→>-<←

Justyna managed to get into the ghetto before the aktzia started, and with Elsa's help she succeeded in escorting her mother out of the ghetto to Bochnia.[49] She stayed with her mother till evening, waiting for Mira, who was supposed to bring her parents on the next train, and for Eva and her parents, who were slated to come last.

Justyna waited for them anxiously. By the time she had left the quarter with her mother it was already difficult to get out, and the ghetto might be sealed off completely at any moment. Once that happened, no Jew would be able to get out. When neither Mira nor Eva showed up, Justyna didn't know what to think. There could be only one possibility: the aktzia had started that very day.

That was a troubling thought. All of the fighters, including Dolek, Marek, Romek, and Maniek, were expecting the aktzia to take place on Wednesday, so they had decided to stay in the ghetto until Tuesday evening. If the aktzia had taken them by surprise and they had all been captured, the backbone and therefore the future of the movement would have been wiped out. Her heart pounding, Justyna returned to Krakow the next morning. She looked around the streets nervously. If anything unusual were going on, she would have felt a change in the atmosphere—something different about the flow. It was a beautiful, sunny day, and though it was autumn, the sun's rays were still strong. Life in Krakow was proceeding at its normal pace. There was no hint of anything unusual happening in the quarter. Justyna noticed nothing different in people's behavior. As she turned a corner, she bumped into Mira, who was wearing a bright fall coat and a brown hat. She was standing on the street, looking around helplessly.

"What's going on, Mirushka?" Justyna sensed that this was no time for elaborate greeting and hugging.

"Nothing," she answered in her resonant alto voice. "The aktzia is in full swing."

---

49. Elsa is Elsa Lapa.

"So it's happening, after all," thought Justyna. She felt a lump in her throat.

"What are you doing, Mira?" she asked.

"To tell you the truth, I don't know. Yesterday evening, at the last minute, I got my parents out of the quarter. We spent the night in some factory. Now I've to get them out of there, but I don't know where to take them. I have an address here. Maybe I'll be able to rent a room at this address and take them there. What bothers me most is that I don't know where Dolek is."

"What do you mean, you don't know?"

"I mean I just don't know."

"Is he in the quarter?"

"I think he and Eva left last night, but I don't know where they went."

They stood there a moment without speaking. Then Justyna asked, "What about the others?"

"Some of them made it to Alek's place."

"Who?" Justyna couldn't believe that the aktzia was actually taking place and that thousands of people would be swept away again. They simply couldn't afford to lose anyone in the movement. Trembling, she waited for Mira to answer.

"Look!" Mira cried out suddenly. The expression on her face changed. "Look, they're coming."

Justyna followed her gaze. A long row of Jewish working women was walking in file along the road. Their faces were pale, their eyes sunken, their steps quick but heavy. An ominous silence hung over them.

"Where are they going?" Mira was pale as a sheet.

"Let's get behind the door," said Justyna. "Some one might recognize us."

"Look over there. Do you see Toska?"[50]

Toska was marching in the second row, erect, her head held high, her rich, dark hair flowing around her shoulders.

"If we could only talk to her for a minute to find out who, where, how."

---

50. Toska is Towa Stark.

"Let's wait inside this alcove till she passes," Justyna urged. "There's no use taking unnecessary risks right now."

[BREAK IN THE TEXT]

"I don't know anything."

"But what's going on inside? How did you manage to get chosen for work?"

"They assembled us in front of the huge building that houses the employment office. All the workers in the ghetto. We were divided according to place of work. Later, a committee went through the rows and picked people for work."

"On what basis?"

"On the basis of whatever they felt like doing."

"And the rest?"

"The rest are going to Zgody Place and then to a transport."

"How many are they taking?"

"One in ten will survive."

"What's it like inside, with everything that's going on?"

"Complete silence."

"No incidents?"

"None."

"Do you have to go now, Toska?"

"I've got to."

"Listen. There are documents for everyone at Alek's place. Get out of the quarter as soon as you have the chance. You'll get the right papers. Alek will tell you whatever you need to know."

"Be well, and take care of yourselves!"

"You keep well, too, and don't give up. Get out of the ghetto as soon as you can."

Toska turned back one more time, scrutinized their grim faces, and then slipped out of the alcove, shutting the door behind her.

→>-<←

"Mirush, come to Alek's after you find a room for your folks. I'll be waiting there for Marek."

It wasn't far to Alek's place. He lived in a small room with an entrance facing the backyard. He was only subletting the place, which was nothing more than a tiny niche with space for a bed and a night table. Since daylight never penetrated the apartment, a small bulb was kept burning day and night. A dark curtain divided one corner from the rest of the room, and it was behind this curtain that the life of the movement was carried on in all its intensity. Vital business was conducted here, and operatives picked up crucial orders. Newcomers made their first contact with the movement in this tiny room, which was always crowded. You had to sit on the bed because there was no space for chairs. People had to rotate in shifts — one entered and another left. Everything had to be said in whispers and all conversation would stop when the door opened, because you never knew who might be coming in. Justyna was struck by the silence behind the curtain when she entered the room. She was afraid nobody would be there, and opened the curtain with trepidation.

Alek, Ziggy, Czesiek, and Adas were sitting on the bed. A heavy pall hung over them. No one spoke. A moment later Marek came in. Though he rarely showed his emotions, the present situation had left its mark even on his stoic, manly face. His blue eyes had grown darker, and his complexion had taken on a grayish cast. His lips were taut, his dark eyebrows drawn together. His high forehead was deeply furrowed. He hadn't slept all night.

→►◄←

With so much work to be done, Marek had gone to Rabka in the evening and worked through the night, preparing documents for those who would be leaving the quarter. He had had to do everything himself, because Justyna was busy making arrangements for her mother. Not knowing the work, Hanusha could be of little assistance. Then Marek washed, freshened up, and returned to Krakow early in the morning. When he got to Alek's, he found out that he had hurried for nothing. The ghetto had been sealed off the previous afternoon, but Dolek, Eva, and Romek had left at the last moment. They were convinced that they wouldn't be able to escape without using their weapons. But somehow they had succeeded in slipping out of the ghetto without any shooting. They had hidden in a warehouse and were still there. Except for them and this little group sitting on the bed right now, everyone was still in the quarter.

Marek couldn't sit still. Since Justyna would not be returning to Podhale, there was no point in his going back there, and since he was unable to contact Romek and Dolek, he took a streetcar and rode around the city. As the streetcar passed the bridge on the Vistula and drew closer to the ghetto, Marek listened intently but heard nothing. All was quiet. No shots, no screams, not even lamentations. Nevertheless, the aktzia was going full tilt. From a distance you could see a thick cordon of gendarmes surrounding the quarter. Everything was taking place almost without a sound, but this was nothing to wonder at. Everything was proceeding according to routine. Everyone had grown accustomed to their designated roles: some to point the accusing finger, some to die, and the rest to endure without complaint.

The streets were empty except for the two spots where the aktzia was concentrated — the area in front of the huge building that housed the employment office, where people were being divided into the able-bodied and those who could not work, and Zgody Place, where they brought those consigned to death. Here they had already assembled the hordes of the condemned. They put the children into one line, the old people into another, and then divided the adults into male and female. The square was crowded with people, thousands of them. A heavy, grave-like stillness hovered over them, like an apparition of death.

→>-<+

That is what an aktzia looked like in Krakow. Death and deportation had the same face here as elsewhere in occupied Poland, but this was a capital city on which the eyes of the world were focused. So in this aktzia, murder had to be committed under the cloak of "resettlement." Hence violence took place without screams, coercion without a shot being fired. Elsewhere, in the provinces, the raging mobs could feast, as they did in Tarnow, where all the Jews were chased into the marketplace and kept kneeling for hours. People's knees grew swollen, but they were forbidden to stand up. Children were torn out of their mothers' arms and lined up in a row off to the side. The machine gun stood ready. Then it was set in motion. The bodies of the children lay on the ground in streams of blood. Their mothers and fathers were kneeling some distance away, and somehow the ground did not cave in under them. Or, on those occasions when the Germans found a large family, they took them all out to the yard, lined them up against the wall, and finished them off in one burst of machine-gun fire. Every yard, gate, and sidewalk was stained with the blood of mothers and children. Long convoys of heavy trucks lumbered along the local roads, piled high with quivering corpses and the wounded, still in agony.

It is difficult to imagine how those who had missed dying by the bullet managed to retain their sanity after witnessing this blood-curdling spectacle, how they could go on living in the horror that hung over the city for days. Yet the silence that hung over the Krakow Ghetto was equally hard to bear. There was more dread in the silence than in groans and despairing laments. Seeing the nerve-shattering routine of people going meekly and passively to the assembly place fanned the flames of inner rebellion.

When Marek got back to Alek's apartment, he was thoroughly shaken. He had been able to observe only fragmented scenes from the streetcar, but based on what he had seen and now reported, they could imagine what was taking place inside the houses and in the unseen streets. They were tormented with concern for the young movement people who had not had a chance to leave the ghetto.

The next day they were to find out the unpleasant facts. The aktzia had struck like lightning. In the course of a single day, the Germans had deported seven thousand people. Those who had an opportunity to hide did so. Of those who were rounded up, some were able to sneak out, while others jumped off the tailgate of a truck at the last minute.

Poldek had ensured the survival of his unit by keeping the young fighters moving from basement to basement. Though they had spent the day eluding one snare after another, some fell victim in spite of their efforts. First of all, Maniek had been deported. Having put too much faith in his working papers, he went directly to the committee instead of going into hiding. That was it for him. Then they took Manusia. Having been saved by a miracle in Warsaw, she had now been caught in Krakow, in her brother's apartment. And after her came Freda. She had been under orders to leave the ghetto and head for the forest the day before the aktzia, but she had delayed because her elderly grandfather had objected to her going, fearing for her safety. He had implored her not to take any unnecessary risks, so she had decided to please the old man by staying a few days longer. She paid for that decision with her life.

What about the others? No one was untouched. Here a brother, last of the family. There a sister, a twin. Mothers, fathers. The aktzia left its bloody imprint on every doorstep. Seven thousand people remained in the quarter. There was mourning in every household. No one doubted any more that everyone in the ghetto was doomed.[51]

In spite of this, life in the quarter went back to normal the next day.

→>-◄-

They were free! The last ties binding them to everyday life had been severed. Following this aktzia, those who had hesitated to join the movement because of responsibility for a younger brother, an only sister, or elderly parents now felt that their chains had been broken and they were free to plunge into the work without second thought. Yet in spite of this heady freedom that blossomed from the ruins of family life, it was still no easy matter for those whose feelings were basically dead to enter into the struggle.

Their consciences were plagued by a host of tormenting questions. "Why wasn't I ready to act sooner?" "Why did it take the death of loved ones to set me free?" Those questions cut more deeply still into the hearts of those behind prison walls, who had to endure long hours with nothing to do but search for answers.

Those who remained free, however, threw themselves into a whirlwind of activity that gave them little time for introspection.

---

51. In the early stages of extermination, the task of selecting individuals to be resettled was imposed on the Jewish Council, and in general they deported those who were not able to do productive work. In the final stages, the S.S. would pick people up arbitrarily in roundups in order to fill quotas of Jews to be deported.

They did not have many moments to spend in contemplation. They tried to drown their intense pain in work so demanding it would numb their feelings. One after another they announced their readiness, and there was certainly more than enough work for everyone.

October was coming to an end in an exceptionally beautiful fall. The leaves held onto their green freshness well into the season. The sun turned the earth to gold, warming it with benevolent rays. Each one of those days was a glorious gift, since at any moment the sky could become overcast and the rain could start falling. Bad weather and muddy autumn days were just around the corner.

One had to prepare for this. Having gone through two difficult experiences in the forest, the leaders realized that this wasn't a good time to search for new territory. It was too late in the season; if they were going to start from scratch, it would be better to do so in the spring. Fall and winter would present insurmountable obstacles to working in an unfamiliar area.

So a new strategy was worked out. Since they were entrenched in the capital city, why seek action in distant places? They could operate right here, which would relieve them of having to build a large apparatus in the forest. Even a minor attack here would strike at the heart of authority and could damage an important cog in the machine. This was their new goal. In the forest it was possible to launch more massive attacks, and little could be accomplished with small groups. But here in the city, an incident staged by one person or a two-man team could raise havoc with the authorities. It would do much more than stir up a bit of anxiety.

They had to shake the self-confidence of those in charge, to demonstrate that the masses were not without spirit and would not accept the government's bestiality, and that the downtrodden were finally rousing themselves from their torpor. The people's spring was about to begin.

Here and there, rational voices advised them not to provoke the government. They recommended building up the movement's strength secretly while lulling the government into believing that nothing was afoot. Why arouse their suspicions with token acts of resistance that would only be irritating at best? But the leaders ignored this advice, for it was based on the assumption that they would survive until spring. Death stalked them daily, and there was no assurance that they could avoid it. They were determined to act now, so that the enemy would feel their wrath. They decided to throw the first roll of the dice in Krakow and to move from there to other large cities.

But to begin with, there was plenty to do inside the ghetto. It was essential to settle scores with the traitors in the ghetto, those who had sold their own brothers for a few pieces of silver or for guarantees of safety. Some were accountable for the murder of hundreds of Jews. For an entire year, the ghetto's population had lived in constant dread of the night raids, when the police went from house to house, working from lists compiled with the aid of collaborators, picking up innocent people for slaughter. The youth movement vowed that as soon as opportunity allowed, they would kill the traitors and their accomplices.

They decided to keep one base in the ghetto and another outside. They also established contact points in the larger cities along the Krakow-Lvov and Krakow-Warsaw lines, and surrounded Krakow with a network of apartments throughout the nearby provinces.

The leadership began to move out of the Krakow ghetto gradually, realizing this was their last chance to get out. Most people in the ghetto knew who they were by then, and whispered from ear to ear that they were sending groups of fighters into the forest. Their names were spoken with reverence, for they had come to represent an ideal of freedom that people longed for with all their souls. But as their popularity grew, their names also came to the attention of the wrong types, the Jewish police, who served the occupying forces better than their own people.

Eva set up a place in Wisnicz, a small, rented house in which she and Dolek and Halina took up residence. Dolek got right down to work, spending the days in Krakow and returning to Wisnicz at night.

Romek also changed apartments. Thanks to his wide circle of acquaintances, Czesiek was able to find an apartment in Krakow's German sector, where he and Romek took up residence.

A few days after the aktzia, two telegrams arrived, both saying more or less the same thing. One was addressed to Nurse Anna at the hospital, and the other to Marek's place. The message went as follows: "I have no means of livelihood. Maniek."

At first, everyone was stunned, but as soon as the shock wore off, all felt a surge of pure joy. They had already counted Maniek among the dead. But he had managed to save himself and was living in Rzeszow. Hela was immediately dispatched to his aid with money and documents. Two days later she brought him, safe and sound, to Krakow. He had jumped out of a sealed boxcar about twenty miles past Rzeszow. He was slightly injured and his face was bruised, but he was able to drag himself to Rzeszow and telegraph Marek and Anna, letting them know where he was.

Now that the leadership was reunited, the work resumed at full speed. Each fighter had a well-defined job that kept him or her on the run from dawn till dusk for days on end, whether it was making inquiries, working as a courier, doing technical work, or actually confronting the enemy. The routine kept everyone busy. Though driven by work and usually exhausted by the end of the day, the fighters headed home in the evening with satisfaction at what had been accomplished, and when one stepped across his threshold, it was with a heart overflowing with happiness. This might well be the last home each would ever know in this life, the last home where the most sacred human feelings could be permitted to burst into the open and rise heavenward in a pure flame. They all felt a tremendous need to love and be loved, a longing for a communal life permeated with closeness. No matter how many times the fire might be extinguished, an even brighter flame replaced it. Time after time the vicissitudes of war had reduced the hot flames to embers. Yet the faint sparks flared up again, and their mutual devotion would be renewed with even greater fervor.

Marek and Dolek started staying overnight in the quarter more frequently, and Romek was particularly loathe to venture into the city. One evening when Dolek didn't return to Wisnicz, Eva and Halina received a visit from a contingent of local police. It was a highly unpleasant attempt at extortion in which the group's spokesman kept beating around the bush. When nothing came of the attempt, the police left, thoroughly embarrassed. The next night they got good and drunk and returned with their newly acquired Dutch courage. This time they happened to find Antek there.

They recognized him immediately, having known him from childhood. Now there was no choice. The matter had to be hushed up, and the movement people had to withdraw before the matter came to the attention of the authorities. They packed their things immediately and returned to Krakow. They had to start searching without delay for an apartment in a different area.[52]

At the same time, the leadership found itself overwhelmed with work, which meant they were tied down to one place. They worked without pause, but each completed task created a new one. Although they were more than willing to keep working at this frenetic pace, there was just too much to be done. They were involved in several activities simultaneously, believing that this would keep the authorities guessing and add to their apprehension. These were truly extraordinary times for the leaders. No matter what the authorities did, they found it impossible to quench the flame of insurrection. There was always one more spark glowing in the deepest recesses of the soul, a flickering ember that would not die. When the fighters were reunited after a difficult episode, the spark would glow ever stronger until it flamed anew with passionate collective commitment.

After the latest aktzia, many houses in the Krakow Ghetto were missing some of their former inhabitants. Many young people found themselves alone in the world, without parents or siblings and with little property to their names. Most often they lived in a sparsely furnished single room. To increase their mobility, they had to convert their inheritance from deported parents into money or to liquidate it in some other way. As a result, a new fashion called "ar-

---

52. What happens in this incident is that after Dolek, Eva, and Halina have set up their apartment in an "Aryan" sector of Wisnicz, local non-Jewish police come sniffing around in an attempt to see if they can extract some bribe money from a group of newly arrived and therefore suspicious strangers. They don't know the two Jewish women who are passing as Aryans, and the women's cheeky behavior throws them off the scent temporarily. The next night the militia men tank up on alcohol and return, still hoping to eke out a bribe. This second night, Antek happens to be paying a visit to the Wisnicz apartment. Apparently, Antek had grown up in Wisnicz, and the policemen, who have known him from childhood, recognize him immediately; of course they know he is a Jew. Now the fighters have been compromised, and it is not clear whether or not they pay the bribe. At any rate, they have been discovered and can no longer operate from the Wisnicz apartment.

ranging a liquidation" came into vogue. The practice got started at Simek's apartment. Simek was one of those whose parents had been deported.[53] All the young people brought whatever had been left in their households to Simek's place: underwear, clothes, boots, valuables—in short, whatever could be redistributed among themselves or sold to raise money for the common cause. After the goods had been gathered and put on display, the redistribution started. Each participant announced his needs and was given the articles he needed. So the possessions of each became the property of all. All distinctions among individuals, which in any event had been growing slighter and slighter, now disappeared.

A common cashbox was set up, followed by a common kitchen. The feeling of homelessness slowly receded. The warmth of family life, which had been wrenched from their lives, was replaced with a new kind of warmth, a different sort of affection, a bond based not on blood ties but on ties of the soul. The entire group used to gather at mealtimes, which became the most pleasant time of the day. Shortly after the aktzia, they had moved into their so-called permanent headquarters, a small two-room apartment that became their home. It was a first-floor apartment with the entrance off a long, narrow corridor.

As you approached the door, you would hear the joyful murmur of youthful voices. No sooner did you open the door a crack than you were enveloped in a warm circle of laughter and lively conversation. Elsa was always in the kitchen, busy at the stove. She cooked, managed, ruled, and complained without end. She reminded everyone of a harried mother hen for whom nothing seemed to go right. The coals hadn't been cut, the water hadn't been fetched, or else the fire refused to burn properly. And then the ungrateful youngsters would form a tight ring around the oven, put their hands on their hips, and poke fun at the angry mother hen. Unable to sustain her anger, Elsa would burst into deep, throaty laughter. That healthy, rugged girl could really laugh.

Everything about Elsa was hardy: her laughter, her tears, her sad-

---

53. Szymon (Simek) Lustgarten's apartment at 13 Jozefinska Street was the headquarters of the Jewish Fighting Organization in the Krakow Ghetto.

ness, her happiness. She was an elemental, high-spirited character. When she tackled a problem, she did it with such abandon that she seemed to lose her capacity to distinguish the essential from the trivial. She would go on about minor details with such intense emotion that they would appear to be matters of life and death. But as soon as she resolved the problem, she would be completely happy again. Her healthy good humor would burst to the surface, and her laughter would ring through that long corridor. Beneath that effervescent demeanor lay a truly courageous soul. When she wanted to help someone, she could move mountains. And she was always ready to help anyone in need. At the moment, she had dedicated her life and soul to the kitchen at Jozefinska 13. She believed that the survival of the universe depended on her kitchen management, so when the young ones surrounded her at the stove and mocked her singlemindedness, she just knitted her brows, chased them out of the kitchen, and carried on with her housekeeping.

The kitchen was so tiny that the stove, tables, and supplies had to be crowded in, and the pots and pans were stacked on the floor. Equipment took up every inch of floor space; when the door was opened even slightly, everything had to be moved. Anyone who wanted to enter the kitchen knew he would have to pick his way carefully through the pots and pans. Each time this ritual was enacted, gales of laughter would break out around the room, and then without warning everyone would start cleaning to get the apartment back in order. In the kitchen, they carried out Elsa's orders obediently. She was a demon for cleanliness and order above all. She swept and scrubbed the floors and cleaned constantly, without any apparent effort. People were always trying to tease her, but they never succeeded in getting her goat, since anger was an emotion alien to her. She would only smile, confused, and instead of lashing out at them would timidly request, "Won't you please wipe your feet before coming into the house? Won't you ever understand?" Then she'd grab the broom and continue sweeping. She spent entire days running in circles.

Simek also played an important part here. He had assumed the role of the traditional head of the household, and revealed a real knack for that pleasant line of work. He inspected every corner. With his hands in his pockets, he would look into what the others were doing. After he had inspected the apartment thoroughly, he would leave dissatisfied and call out, "This place is a real mess. You've really made an unholy mess this time."

Simek and Nolek were in charge of supplies.[54] They stocked the cupboards and supplied people with whatever they needed. All of their activities took place in a general atmosphere of euphoria. For example, there were articles of clothing left over from the "liquidation auction" lying around. These old-fashioned outfits from bygone eras strewn around the apartment provoked frequent outbursts of mirth.

Whenever Hanusha came from Krakow, she brought all sorts of priceless objects from the liquidation stock for Justyna's household. And of course she also brought warm greetings from that world of intense emotions that comprised the two-room apartment in the Krakow Ghetto.

"Justyna," she once said, "if you only knew how pleasant it is to be there! The moment you walk into the apartment you are at home, among the people closest to you, taking part in the most heartwarming conversations. If you ever went there, you wouldn't want to return to this barren villa in the forest."

"Hanusha," Justyna replied sadly, "is it really so hard for you to stay here with me?"

"No. It's not that I don't enjoy being with you, it's just that I feel sorry for both of us. They enjoy such a rich life in the Ghetto. When they come home from work, it's the way it used to be in Warsaw, and the way it must have been for you in Kopaliny, maybe even better."

It was true. Life really was good at Jozefinska 13. The soul of the movement was concentrated in that apartment, and anyone in the movement who came to Krakow would try to get into the ghetto at any price, just to get a look at the place. Every day at dusk, Alek left his post to go there. Czesiek would crawl out of his hiding place so he could visit, and Romek used to sneak in whenever possible.

In that way everyone who lived in the apartment met those passing through, some with whom they'd been in frequent contact, others from whom they'd been separated for years. It is difficult to

---

54. Nolek is Nathan Parizer.

understand how people who were so oppressed could still experience such joy. Who knows, perhaps all the love that would have been given to their murdered families had been displaced onto their comrades, and perhaps this love was deepened further by the tragic premonition that they were now ensconced in the last home they would ever inhabit.

Perhaps they felt that this house was not only the last home they would know, but the last place where the flame of Jewish cultural life could still burn brightly. Perhaps they believed this was the last time they could live in a group as themselves, without effacing their Jewish identities.

They had absorbed and nurtured within themselves all the values of their people and had rejuvenated the old traditions; in short, they were living a distinctly Jewish life in a distinctly Jewish atmosphere. Dolek often dropped in, and whenever he showed up, a group gathered around him. Then the evening grew both more festive and more pensive. At these times an inexplicable beauty would hover over the room. Those evenings were so extraordinary and so sacred that they touched the souls of those present and would never be erased from memory.

The apartment kept getting more and more crowded, because although some people left on assignments, they were more than replaced by the ones who kept coming. During the day the door was in constant motion, and at night the problem became one of how to provide lodging for everyone. Two extra double beds were set up, each of which was regularly occupied by six or seven young people. They also improvised by making beds on the floor and on chairs. Every corner was put to use for the night. Though sanitary conditions were poor and even the most primitive conveniences were lacking, no one thought of leaving for lack of physical comforts. What they found in that apartment was dearer than the most expensive luxuries and far more satisfying.

The house on Jozefinska became the movement's base of operations, an assembly point where people checked in and from which they were dispatched to combat posts. Every evening they would sneak out in twos or threes. Some had been assigned the job of taking out traitors and sell-outs inside the quarter, while others were given the task of finding weapons on the outside. The minute before

curfew they came running into the apartment, short of breath —
sometimes exulting in their successes, sometimes frustrated at having come close to accomplishing their goals but falling short. Several
times they had miraculously slipped out of a police dragnet. Often it
seemed one of them was about to get a bullet squarely in the head,
and only managed to escape with his life by a quick dodge or zigzag.

One evening Ziggy, Dolek, and Czesiek went out on a job. The
plan was for Czesiek to bring a German sergeant of the guard, a
"friend" of his, to a spot where Ziggy and Dolek would be waiting in
ambush, concealed by the darkness at the bank of the Vistula. When
Czesiek and his prey failed to arrive at the appointed time, the
youths started getting edgy. They were burning to act, and in their
eagerness kept clutching the weapons in their pockets. They waited,
but Czesiek did not show up.

Suddenly a shot was fired, and Ziggy slumped to the ground.
Dolek looked around but didn't see anyone. Who had fired the shot?
In a flash he grasped what had happened. Out of nervousness and
frustration, Ziggy had squeezed the trigger. The bullet had entered
his knee, plowed down his leg underneath the skin, and emerged
without touching the bone.

Ziggy lay motionless. As Czesiek had not yet returned, Dolek was
on his own. He had to act fast to get Ziggy out of there before
someone saw him. Fortunately, there was no one else around. Dolek
helped Ziggy up quickly. Biting his lip in pain, Ziggy got to his feet.
As he took his first step, leaning on Dolek's shoulder, he felt un-
bearable pain. They had no time to waste. Waiting for Czesiek to
show up was out of the question. Nor was there any point in pretending they could get anything else done that night. With super-
human effort, they dragged themselves into the quarter just before
curfew. When they entered Number 13, everyone was shocked at
Ziggy's ghostly demeanor. The noise and laughter stopped abruptly.

The girls prepared a place for Ziggy to lie on, then eased him
down. The wound was serious. The leg was bleeding profusely. They
had to get a doctor, yet didn't dare let anyone in on their secret. They
sent for Anna first, but a simple dressing wasn't enough to stop the
bleeding and ease the pain. Even an injection of painkiller didn't
help. The wound had to be sutured. There was no alternative. Finally, they decided to call in a female surgeon they felt they could

trust. It was nine o'clock when the doctor arrived. She had brought two policemen for her own protection.[55] The situation became unpleasant as the policemen looked around the room inquisitively.

How come there were so many young people in such a small apartment? This wound — what kind of an accident had caused it?

To satisfy their curiosity, the fighters told a tale about an accident at work. The police listened incredulously, nosing around the apartment, and insisted on taking a look at the wound. Only with the greatest difficulty were they dissuaded from doing so.

When the surgery was completed and the police had finally left, everyone breathed a sigh of relief. They tiptoed around the apartment, trying not to disturb Ziggy. An unusual silence descended on both rooms. The wounded lad fell asleep. They guarded him with tremendous vigilance. He was dearer to them now than ever.

→>~<←

By the time Czesiek arrived at the rendezvous place, it was almost nine o'clock. Finding no one there, he became apprehensive. Nothing seemed to be going right this time. His own mission had failed miserably. The duty officer he was supposed to bring along had been too busy to accompany him into town, so Czesiek's whole evening had been wasted. Now his frustration mounted because he had no idea what had happened to Dolek and Zygmunt. Czesiek walked around the boulevard a few times, whistling to signal that he had arrived. Receiving no answer, he looked at his watch again. Nine o'clock.

He cursed under his breath and took off for home. He had decided to return to his own apartment that night instead of going to the quarter. Maybe tomorrow he would find out what had happened. But how? Perhaps Alek would know something, but since Czesiek was already under suspicion, he couldn't be seen walking the streets during the day. The next day he was very worried and was feeling rotten about having wasted the previous evening. Yet he was cooped up in his apartment, unable to do anything. The next day, as evening

---

55. Here Draenger is referring to the Jewish police.

fell, he went to Number 13. When he saw his friend lying there wounded, he was deeply distressed and sat on the bed next to him. Neither one spoke. The others moved around the apartment soundlessly, still in shock because of the accident.

Though a deep sadness had settled on Jozefinska 13, the work continued nonetheless. The momentum was so powerful that nothing could slow them down. So they continued to forge ahead at full throttle.

None of the fighters will ever forget those thrilling times — those evenings spent hunting down traitors or prowling around, looking for action; those times they lay in ambush behind a coal bin, and the times they attacked the enemy in dark alleys.

The work of the movement became all-consuming. Although they had not been brought up to do this kind of work, they gave themselves over to it heart and soul. The only time any of them felt satisfied now was when he was carrying out an assignment on a dark night, a weapon pressed tightly in his hand.

Those evenings were unforgettable. You would drop into Number 13 and utter one short word: "Ready!"

Later that night, everyone would be exhilarated by a sense of accomplishment, and the adrenalin would be running too high for anybody to sleep. The next day the authorities would scour the city, looking for the culprits, who were holed up here in the middle of the ghetto, right under the noses of the police, walking the streets with impunity and laughing with contempt at the fruitless police searches.

But in spite of their high spirits, they were deeply scarred. First, they were ever mindful of the three who had gone in search of the golden fleece and never returned. They didn't delude themselves about the missing trio. Edwin, Emil, and Harry were gone for good, and nobody even knew how they had died. They had vanished without a trace, a thought so unsettling that in itself it sufficed to rob the fighters of their peace of mind forever. They tried not to talk about it, but deep in their souls they kept repeating the words, "They'll never return. They'll never return."

An air of quiet dignity now permeated the apartment at Jozefinska 13, but even this serenity could not dissipate the sense of sadness, which was further deepened by the fact that Zygmunt was gravely ill. He was cared for lovingly, and his bed became the center of life in the apartment. Every few minutes someone would approach his bed and speak softly to him, just long enough to make his enforced rest more bearable, but not so long as to tire him.

The girls outdid each other in caring for him. They cooked him a variety of meals, and brought him fruit and other delicacies. After a while, they started competing with each other, not so much for Ziggy's sake as to see who would prove herself the best nurse. The hands-down winners of this competition were Stasia and Giza, who became his surrogate mothers, as they were jokingly called.[56] The pain was still so severe that Ziggy couldn't drag himself out of bed, but the initial shock of the errant shot had worn off. The good-humored joking and banter gradually resumed. Conversations grew louder, and laughter rang out more often. The voices in the apartment sounded happier from day to day.

Ziggy was slowly returning to his old self. He had been suffering guilt at the thought of having become a burden to his mates because of his own carelessness. But in this warm and loving atmosphere his guilt slowly receded, and his usual composure started to reassert itself. Life at Number 13 was just about getting back to normal when they received some good news that boosted their morale considerably and helped lift the pall hanging over them.

One evening Mirka burst into the apartment unexpectedly, her face glowing with a most radiant smile. She could not contain her joy.

"Anka is here," she shouted from the threshold.

"What are you talking about?"

"Where is she?"

"Are you sure you weren't dreaming?"

"If I tell you she's here, she's here!"

"Why didn't she come here with you?"

"She'll come soon. You'll see."

"Tell us how the miracle happened."

"She didn't escape from jail, did she?"

"Tell us how she did it."

---

56. Giza is Gizela Stockhammer.

"Quiet down, and I'll tell you what happened. I'm just getting back from Alek's. I was there because . . . Never mind that, it's not important. I'm at Alek's when all of a sudden the door opens, and in walks Anka. Imagine my surprise. No, this was not just a surprise, an ordinary delight. I don't know what to call it. Anka is alive! She was set free. Just think of it! Without any influence or intervention! She kept up her act right to the end. Finally, they all believed her. They acknowledged that she was being held unjustly. Think of it!"

"How's she feeling now?"

"Completely normal! She's pale and she's grown a little thinner, but she's still herself. In fact, she's returned bursting with energy and wants to get to work immediately. You'll see for yourselves. She'll be here soon."

Anka had become involved in resistance activities soon after the war started, and until recently had been part of a circle made up exclusively of Poles. She had not given much thought to her Jewish identity, and when occasional thoughts of her Jewishness did pop into her mind, she would quickly suppress them. Anka's youthful experience as a Polish scout had left an indelible stamp on her personality. Nevertheless, when she met Mirka for the first time, they were instantly drawn to each other. Their encounter took place at the juncture of two very different worlds, but despite certain differences in attitude, they understood each other quite well. Though Mirka was quite a bit older than Anka, her personal charm attracted Anka, and they soon became the closest of friends.

It was then that Anka started feeling the first stirrings of her Jewish identity. By the time she joined the movement, she had matured considerably and was eager to learn everything without delay. She wanted to get to know the whole organization, to study the history and ideas of her people, to do a tour of duty at every outpost, to make up for all the time she had wasted not knowing what it meant to be a Jew. She was prepared to fight in the front line, to engage in the struggle with all the strength and toughness of her womanly soul.

She had demonstrated her toughness in prison, where she had stuck to her story to the very end. She refused to give in and kept up the pretense so long and so convincingly that she finally threw the bloodhounds off the trail. She was exonerated of the charge of being a Jew, with the jailer himself declaring that she'd been slandered. She had effected her release from prison by sheer strength of will.

As soon as she was released, she hurried back to her home and family. But here another shock awaited her. She had left Krakow without even saying goodbye to her mother, who had been loath to give her only daughter permission to leave. Anka had argued, cajoled, begged, all to no avail, so she had decided to slip away without her mother's permission. She packed a few personal effects, as though she were just going to spend the night with one of her girlfriends, and since her mother wasn't home when she left the house, she kissed her little brother goodbye and departed. She never returned.

Walking through the streets after her departure, she told herself, "I'll return to Krakow in about a week, two at most. Mother will be so happy to see me that she'll forgive me on the spot." This thought had consoled her. How was she to know that the first trap was already waiting to be sprung? Ziggy, who returned from Rozwadow soon after, described seeing her led away by a policeman.

"She walked with such confidence that it seemed she was leading the policeman, and not the reverse."

Her stoic manner remained with her to the end, though she was actually consumed with longing for her mother and brother, whom she feared she would never see again. She thought about them continually, wondering how they were doing without her. When she first got back to Krakow after her release, she hadn't heard about the aktzia in the quarter. On reentering the ghetto, the first thing she did was look for her mother and brother. When she didn't find them, she was stunned. In a daze, she wandered over to Jozefinska 13. She entered the apartment pale as a ghost, still in shock.

Her comrades had been waiting impatiently, and now their sincere delight in greeting her enveloped her in a wave of affection. She felt that she had come back to her people, to the home where she could take a well-deserved rest after the nervous strain of prison. With some difficulty, she detached herself from the warm embraces of her well-meaning friends. When she got to the kitchen, everybody wanted to hug her, or at least to squeeze her hand. As the crowd pressed around, she noticed someone lying in bed in the other room.

"Who's sick?"

"Zygmunt."

She quickly went over and sat next to him on the bed. They conversed privately for a long time while their comrades looked on joyfully. A heavy pain lifted from each heart. Every moment was suffused with good feeling. In each other's presence the two of them experienced a joy more intense than ever. That same week they all spent a supremely beautiful evening celebrating Anka's return. The celebration was planned for a Friday to coincide with the Greeting of the Sabbath.[57] They spent two days preparing the meal and festivities, which would begin at sundown and probably continue till dawn. They anticipated that evening with utmost impatience.

For years they had kept up that tradition that marked the leap from the gray procession of profane time into the radiance of the holy. Hushed by the imminence of the sacred, they waited for the lighting of the candles that would send a sudden glow around the festive room. The girls were dressed in white blouses, and the boys in white shirts with collars open at the throat. Deeply moved, they sat around the table, which was covered with a white cloth. First a moment of silence, and then they would raise a swelling hymn of praise to the Sabbath from their souls. Their eyes, sparkling with candlelight, expressed their passionate yearnings. At such times it seemed as if a more radiant and pure soul had entered each of them.

The members of the youth group had observed this custom for many years. Whether in a quiet village or a bustling city, whether high in the mountains or among factory chimneys, they always greeted the Sabbath-Bride with the same song and the same powerful feelings. This particular evening, in this hallowed circle, they greeted Her as a group for the last time.

They felt no fear for the future. They were so happy that song followed song in a deluge of harmonies, each outburst binding them yet more tightly together. Amid this overflowing happiness, someone called out, "This is the Last Supper."

The phrase captured their imaginations and embedded itself in their memories. From then on, whenever they talked about that evening, they used that phrase.

---

57. "Greeting of the Sabbath" refers to the Hebrew phrase *Kabbalat Shabbat*, the term for the ritual.

Dolek was seated at the head of the table, surrounded by those faces so dear to him, so filled with radiance and warmth. People were crowded close. Although the room had been full for some time, new arrivals kept coming—and somehow space had to be found. Martusia sat in a corner, staring wide-eyed at Dolek and the faces around him, bright in the flickering candlelight.[58]

This is her first Sabbath away from home. She had escaped from the Tomaszow Ghetto when the aktzia started. She knew she might never see her parents again, her beloved parents, so young in spirit! Bidding her goodbye, her father had said, "If I were a little younger, I'd be going with you."

Marta carried those words with her, buried in her heart, a souvenir second in value only to the memory of her father himself. Since leaving, she has thought of nothing but those parting moments.

She no longer has a home! No place to return to! She has little doubt that her father, mother, and younger sister were swept away by the aktzia. Seventeen years old, she is alone in the world. She stares at her surroundings, feeling no pain, no sadness for her lost home, her childhood, her carefree youth, though she knows they are gone. She has found her place with these young people. Listening to Dolek, she feels a heightening, a glimmering of joy in the crowded room. She has known him for years, but he is saying unfamiliar things. He always generated optimism, uttering strong words that encouraged you to believe in life and love it. But today his words convey that the end is near, and he seems to ask his listeners to confront their fates stoically.

It's as if he can feel death approaching, because he talks about it at length. He no longer believes they will survive, and he doesn't want anyone harboring false hopes. He doesn't want them deluding themselves. He wants those going out on assignments to realize that death is near. He hurls his hard words into the heart of the festive atmosphere.

"We're on a journey of no return. The road we've chosen is the road to death. Remember that. Whoever hopes to survive must not seek survival among us or in our work. We've reached the road's end, but it's not an end that will plunge us into darkness. We're going

---

58. Martusia is Towa Fuchs.

out to face the angel of death, but we'll face him as bold idealists. I have a feeling this is the last time we'll greet the Sabbath together. We have to leave the quarter, because our whereabouts and activities are too well known. This week we'll start to liquidate this oasis we've established at Number 13. One more phase of our lives is about to close, but we can't afford to second-guess ourselves, to regret anything we've done. It couldn't have been any other way."

As the Last Supper drew to a close, a gray dawn peeped in the window.

The following Sunday, Dolek took five new people out on a sortie—Tosca, Marta, Henek, Rena, and Giza.[59] Each was assigned a different spot. Dolek gave final instructions and a sort of fatherly blessing for the road. No, it wasn't exactly a blessing he gave them, but words of encouragement, words to sustain them and serve as a reservoir of strength to draw on for a long time to come. He gave them a pep talk, though one thought kept running through his mind the whole time: "We're going to certain death."

→>‒<‒

Now that the crisis was coming to a head, they could look back at their work and think of it as a polyphonic composition, with the separate melodies fusing into a glorious harmony. The fused harmonic pitches rise higher and higher until they crescendo in a climactic chord, a confluence of reverberating tones. But this flood of sound is only a resting point in the unresolved harmonic flow; A silent pause must follow this resonant chord to give the mighty tones their proper effect. The orchestra is quiet. The artists rest, but the music still echoes in the listeners' ears, the sound waves still vibrate, the vivid tones still hover.

When the climactic chord stops resonating and its last traces fade into silence as if retreating to a far-off place, the violinist takes up his instrument and his bow caresses the hushed strings once more, reviving the suspended melody. At first the awakened melody emerges pianissimo, but as the winding strands start interweaving again, the

---

59. Henek was Henryk Monderer, and Rena, Regina Feurstein.

melodic structure soars once more, climbing ever higher till it re-solves into another climactic chord, after which there must be an-other pause and another silence. This is what the movement's work was like.

As I write these words, many fighters are still living. These are fighters who jump from a dark alley, deliver a blow, confiscate a weapon, then disappear in the thick of night; some distribute printed flyers on busy streets, trying to rouse people from their apathy; oth-ers work like moles, spying on the secret police, doing their part in defending the seed of freedom; all carry out their assignments fear-ing nothing in this world, desiring nothing more than an honorable death. Many of us now await this very death behind the walls of this prison. Since the investigation is in process, every word I utter can still influence the fate of those using their freedom to carry on the work. So I must restrain myself. I am not yet at liberty to tell every-thing these fearless youths have accomplished.

Every evening was crowned with heroic exploits, and each exploit thundered a resounding "No!" in the ears of those who had ap-pointed themselves masters of life and death over millions of de-fenseless people. Some evenings were more rewarding than others. As they became more experienced, the fighters operated more pre-cisely and efficiently. Each successive incident seemed to bring them closer to some critical culmination, some unseen turning point.

It was early November, when the nights were already quite long and a thick fog covered the earth. Somewhere in the park, three fighters — Dolek, Jendrek, and Stefek — were hidden in the bushes. They were all first-rate. Jendrek had come to the fore recently. He had been one of Justyna's students. She'd always had great faith in him, though from his early youth she had seen him as an incorrigible cynic. He revealed his cynicism in his sarcasm toward all ideals, his indifference to other people's enthusiasms, and the very expression on his face. Although Justyna despised cynicism, she believed nev-ertheless that somehow, some day, Jendrek's cynicism would take a constructive and creative turn. No one could understand this para-dox, not even Justyna. But though she couldn't explain it, she con-tinued to believe in it. When Jendrek had left the movement, the members of his platoon gently informed Justyna that their hopes had gone up in smoke. Yet Justyna continued to think of Jendrek as one of her people and waited for his return. Years later he did return, and just in time. Now his cynicism had actually become a virtue, for it enabled him to carry out whatever work was assigned him with the utmost cold-bloodedness.

Stefek was another late arrival on the scene who had recently returned to the movement. No one knew quite what to think of him. He was silent as a tomb, which made him appear a mature man of deep wisdom and strong character. He was all the more intimidating because of his healthy, powerful physique. Yet at times his reticence made the leaders hesitant to trust him. But ultimately he turned out to be a conscientious fighter who made himself indispensable. When there was serious and demanding work to be done, it was assigned only to the strongest, most reliable operatives. The mission they had planned this time was momentous. Today they would attempt to strike the climactic chord.

They didn't have to wait long to test their plan. No sooner had they taken their positions in the bushes than they heard the heavy boot-steps. The sergeant's large figure appeared in the darkness. To them he represented all the arrogance, viciousness, and sadism of the brutal regime. He was a symbol of the unbridled evil that had to be eradicated from the world. All the suppressed anger and resentment that had festered in them for months erupted with irrepressible force. One quick volley and that personification of evil lay in a pool of blood. Tightly clutching their contraband weapons, they mixed with the crowds. Nobody noticed them. People in the streets panicked and started running in all directions, scared by the sound of gunfire, thinking only of their own safety, worried that the authorities might implicate them in the deed.

Our trio walked home calmly. To throw any pursuers off their trail, they returned along a zig-zag route through a web of side streets. They were safe. No one had followed them. When Dolek arrived home, he complained of a splitting headache. Perhaps he was feigning it to get a few quiet moments to himself. He lay down on the couch, and everyone left the room quietly.

The city came to a boil. This last act was more than the authorities could tolerate. They felt that the underground was gaining strength, that the resistance was taking on the dimensions of a significant fighting force. They would have to crush the rebellion at birth. They would have to strangle the Hydra before she could lift her head any higher. Oh, how they hated those youngsters who had reared up to carry out this deed. How frightened they were! Their fear knew no bounds!

How embarrassing it was to have to acknowledge that someone dared resist. How ashamed they were of being compelled to admit that a secret network flourished that they had not yet managed to crush. Although the authorities had the newspapers report in banner headlines the story of a hero fallen in the line of duty, they also circulated conflicting rumors: the sergeant had been murdered by a band of unknown hooligans, or he had committed suicide for some unknown reason.

New versions of the event kept emerging, including stories about a secret underground, but the authorities did their best to present the incident as a street brawl or the result of some personal intrigue. The fact that the authorities beefed up their security arrangements showed for the first time how much they respected their underground adversary. These new precautions indicated beyond doubt that they considered their enemy a legitimate threat.

Curfew time on the Aryan side was moved up two hours, from eleven P.M. to nine. Fear gripped the populace. The streets emptied before dark; people ran home in a panic as soon as they had finished their errands. The streets were patrolled more frequently, and passersby were scrutinized more closely. The police stopped people at random and searched them thoroughly, adding to the panic.

The repressive measures were intended to prevent other such incidents, but the authorities still had to apprehend the culprits, and they intended to do this by whatever means necessary. They started their pursuit of the killers by taking hostages, undoubtedly an effective measure. Out of any twenty people picked up at random in the quarter, there were bound to be several who knew the address. It was inevitable.

Though nobody in the quarter knew the exact details of the movement's operations, and though no one had any idea of the movement's future plans, everyone knew something was brewing. For a cowardly person who felt the knife at his throat, the easiest way out was simply to say, "They're the ones."

It wasn't long before the entire leadership was on the list, even though no leader was ever caught red-handed. As soon as the police had their list, they pressed the hunt with such total dedication that you might have thought they were in quest of the holy grail.

Fortunately, the leadership sensed the danger in time. They decided to leave the quarter and go underground. It was not that they were frightened. On the contrary, the current struggle warmed their blood. They felt the time approaching when they would have to engage in an open fight, and they were actually happy about it. Their spirits soared. They devised a detailed plan to be put into effect the following morning. That night they would remain in concealment at their usual addresses. They treated the whole affair casually, not expecting the police to be in any great hurry.

That evening Eva returned from one of her trips so tired she barely had enough energy to greet Dolek. All she wanted to do was lie down and rest.

Dolek was about to leave the house. He had decided to spend the night at his mother's. The apartment was unoccupied, because after the last aktzia his parents had decided to remain outside the quarter. Mira was away on a trip to Radom to establish contact with the outpost where Sabina was working, so there was plenty of room in his parents' apartment.

"Are you coming with me?"

"Why? Where are you going?" Eva asked, somewhat surprised. She listened silently as he told her quickly what had happened while she was away. Then he asked her again, "What are you going to do?"

"I'll stay here. I'm utterly exhausted. I'm not going anywhere right now because I don't have the strength. After all," she added, laughing, "nothing's going to happen today."

But a lot did happen. As soon as Dolek left, Eva fell sound asleep. The accumulation of several days of fatigue had finally caught up with her and knocked her right off her feet. She didn't even hear the loud knocking on the door. It was only nine-thirty when ten policemen came storming into the room, and she didn't even hear them. They entered triumphantly, having already accomplished one part of their assignment — barely a minute ago they had taken Maniek to the police station. Assuming that nothing would happen, Maniek had stayed at home, where the police apprehended him. As their enterprise had been so successfully launched, they entered the apartment with great self-assurance. At first Eva continued to sleep soundly, but finally the commotion woke her. As she jumped out of bed, she happened to look in Arthur's direction.[60] He was an old acquaintance from school who'd been her partner at one of the dramatic evenings. He could hardly be called a close friend, but they'd had some good times together, and he had once been an admirer. Since becoming a high-ranking policeman, he had taken to dropping in to see her frequently. They had talked openly to each other. The leaders had trusted him, hoping to win him over to the movement. He was on the verge of joining, but just couldn't bring himself to decide. Perhaps they had pushed him too hard, too soon.

When Eva's eyes met his, she thought, "I'll get out of this somehow. After all, it's only Arthur."

At that same moment Arthur was thinking, "What a pity! She's such a beautiful girl! But it's her tough luck. I can't afford to be sentimental."

Aloud he said, "We've come for Dolek."

"He's not here," came the curt reply.

"Where is he?"

"None of your business."

"You've got to come with us."

"What for?"

"As a hostage."

"All right. I'll come."

She was calm as they took her off to the police station, but they weren't. They had orders to arrest everyone with a certain family name. Next on their list were Dolek's parents. Having secured Eva, the police set off on the hunt once more. The quarter was small; there was no place in the ghetto they couldn't reach within five minutes. In no time they were in front of Dolek's parents' place. The house was shrouded in darkness. Romek and Dolek were asleep on the daybed. They had gone to sleep with a pleasant satisfaction, looking forward to their first open encounter with the police. They could hardly wait for the game to get started.

---

60. Arthur Lefler, a militiaman (*Ordnungsdienstmann*) who tracked members of the Jewish Fighting Organization for the Gestapo.

When the ten uniformed policemen stepped into the room and turned on the lights, Romek and Dolek were sleeping with utter peace of mind. The two woke up and took in the situation at a glance. They didn't say a word, but lay there staring indifferently at the intruders. When Arthur saw Dolek, some remaining tatter of conscience awoke in him. Not expecting to find Dolek here, he found himself psychologically unprepared for the encounter. As he stood there facing Dolek, it began to dawn on Arthur what a pathetic figure he was. In an attempt to regain his composure, he stalled for time. Pretending not to see the men on the daybed, he led the ten policemen into the next room, which was inhabited by a different family. He called out the first and last names of Dolek's parents.

"There's no such party living here."

Now he had no choice but to lead the policemen back into the first room. He screwed up his courage, took a deep breath, and said a little sheepishly, "We've come to take you in, Dolek."

"What made you look for me here?"

"We looked for you in your apartment . . ."

"And?"

"We had to take Eva into custody as a hostage."

"I understand. I'll go with you on the condition that you first let my wife go."

"Good. While you're getting ready, I'll run down to the police station. By the time you get there, Eva will be free."

Arthur left. Dolek leaped out of bed and dressed hastily. Once he had finished dressing, he pretended to adjust minor details of his clothing. In actuality, he was looking for something. Finally he declared himself ready to go.

The police breathed a sigh of relief when he gave himself up voluntarily. They had been so sure he would resist that his apparent compliance took them by surprise. They didn't understand why he had taken so long to get dressed, but they had their man, and that was all they cared about.

They walked into the dark autumn night, their steps echoing loudly in the sleepy quarter, the nine policemen in uniform and Dolek in civilian clothes. Dolek walked slowly, trying to make the trip last as long as possible. He needed time to sort things out. As he

was planning his next step, he noticed Arthur in the distance, returning by himself.

"Where's Eva?"

"They won't release her until you get there."

"So that's how it is," Dolek muttered. Now he realized the situation was serious. They weren't far from the police station. Every
minute could mean life or death. He calculated his chances rapidly.
He had to get Eva out of the station as soon as possible. They would
escape together. He worked out a whole scenario. He would demand
to see his wife under the pretext that he wanted to say goodbye. As
soon as he was with her again, he would fire a shot and they would
make their break.

He could see the station about a hundred steps down the road.
Dolek ran through his plan one more time and realized at the last
moment that he'd miscalculated. The police were unlikely to let
them get close enough for him to tell Eva his plan. They might not let
him see her at all. The first phase of his plan had already fallen apart.
And he had no way of knowing what things would be like inside the
station, or who might be waiting for him. Perhaps it would be impossible to resist by then. Perhaps he shouldn't wait. This might
really be his last chance. If he could make his getaway now, he'd be
able to set Eva free later without too much effort. They could even
organize a raid to free her tomorrow. If he could remain on the
outside, everything would still be possible. He could not surrender
now. Suddenly he stopped in his tracks and put his hand in his
pocket. The ten uniformed men pulled up in surprise. Calmly taking
out his gun, Dolek spoke with calculated composure: "Now boys,
this is your last chance to get out of here alive, because in a second
I'm going to start shooting."

The police were unarmed. Their occupation was one of the most
demeaning imaginable. They served the government, not the people
of the quarter. They had chosen to collaborate with the occupiers
and thus had sold their souls to the devil. Although the authorities
were willing to trust them with the responsibility for suppressing the
people, they did not trust them enough to issue weapons to them. So
the police were equipped with nothing more lethal than a hat and a
rubber bludgeon. They were so despised that they became, predict-
ably, even more sullen and mean-spirited. They did not trust each

other, and while they didn't hesitate to oppress those beneath them with their free-swinging rubber bludgeons, they cowered in the presence of those with authority over them. When they saw a weapon, they trembled with fear.

Upon hearing the words "I'm going to start shooting," they turned to putty. They turned and ran as fast as they could. When they finally reached the safety of the station's doorway, they looked back, and in an attempt to recoup their honor and perhaps to mask the fear that had set them trembling, called out, "Madman! Where do you think you're going?"

But by then Dolek had disappeared into the darkness.

→>-<-

No sooner had the door closed behind the policemen than Romek leaped out of bed and dressed hurriedly. He knew he had been spared only because the policemen were too preoccupied with Dolek to pay attention to anyone else. He had to get out of the apartment, because the police might return any second. He sneaked through the yard, using no light, since he didn't want to draw attention. He squeezed through a hole in the fence, snaked his way through a few gardens, and soon stood in front of Jozefinska 13. His people were still awake, singing songs, telling tales. The nights always seemed too short for them. They felt that fateful moment when they would be separated approaching all too quickly, and they begrudged every minute lost in sleep, since it robbed them of precious time together. They shortened each night to a couple of hours, so their evenings reached into the wee hours of morning, and the singing never seemed to cease.

When they saw Romek standing in the doorway, pale, lips pressed together, they stopped singing abruptly, breaking off in the middle of a song. They looked in alarm as he closed the door behind him without uttering a word. Hands in his pockets, body erect, he walked through the kitchen, all eyes following him. In the next room, he sat down on Ziggy's bed and said nothing for a while, trying to collect his thoughts. He bent close to the wounded man's ear and whispered something to him while those in the other room looked on. They watched a range of emotions flash across Ziggy's face, from astonishment to fear to terror and finally to a self-imposed, disciplined impassivity. The two men consulted briefly, speaking in whispers. Still ignorant of what had happened, the young people waited in suspense. Then Romek got up and called to Marysiu, who was in the kitchen.[61]

She ran into the bedroom, quite pale. Her small, childish face revealed anxiety. Still she squinted charmingly, as she usually did when frightened.

"I'm listening," she said obediently, letting herself down slowly beside the bed.

"You've got to go to Dolek's parents immediately. Do you know where they live?"

"Certainly."

"Don't take a flashlight and don't make a sound. You've got to get there unseen. There's important material hidden there."

"Where is it?"

He described everything in detail. She put on a coat and ran out. A minute later she was at the window of the Markiewicz house.[62] She knocked on the window pane. No answer.

"Dolek," she called softly.

Again, no answer. She knocked once more, loudly this time. A strange face leaned out of the next window.

"Who are you looking for at this hour of the night?"

"The Markiewiczes."

"They're not home."

"I'm looking for their son."

"So, you haven't heard?"

"Heard what?"

"The police took him in about an hour ago."

Marysiu was speechless at first, but regained her composure in an instant and called out, "Would you please let me in? I have to get in there. It's very important that I get in."

As she spoke, they recognized her as someone who used to visit Mirka quite often. They opened the door for her, and in a minute she

---

61. Marysiu is Minka Brenner.

62. Markiewicz was the "Aryan" name used by Dolek's parents.

found everything she was looking for. She packed the material away and returned to Number 13 the same way she had come, through broken fences and across backyards.

By the time she returned, everyone knew that Dolek had been arrested. She could tell, as soon as she walked in, by the bowed heads and the sadness that permeated the apartment. It seemed they had reached the end of the line. She walked up to Romek and handed him the material. Everything was done without a word. They couldn't manage to force a sound out of their throats. An ominous and seemingly interminable silence hung over the room.

Suddenly they were shocked out of their torpor by the sound of footsteps outside. They heard someone run quickly up to the house, then someone else even more quickly. Then a third, and a fourth, and soon it seemed that dozens of people were running back and forth in the yard. The running was punctuated with calls and whistles. In a flash, they figured out what was going on. The thought struck them all at the same instant: the police were looking for Romek. They put out the light and barely dared to breathe. The activity outside grew more frenzied. The calls grew louder. The young people inside realized that there was no point in procrastinating. Their first priority was to conceal Romek. He must be saved, or else. . . . They didn't dare complete the thought. They were too preoccupied with finding a way to keep Romek out of the hands of the police to analyze the situation precisely. They had only one thought: they must save Romek at any price. No matter what happens, he must be saved.

They took the beds apart and put Romek under the mattress, spread a sheet over the mattress, and placed the bedding on top. Two girls lay down on the bed, pretending to be asleep, as if nothing had happened. The rest of them feigned sleep as well. The idea was to make it look as if they were all sleeping peacefully, as on any normal night. But the truth is, no one slept a wink that night. They expected the door to be forced open any minute and a whole division of police to come storming into the house. When that happened, they would let themselves be taken, but they wouldn't betray Romek for anything in the world.

They hadn't a clue that the police were actually after Dolek. When the ten policemen had returned to the station empty-handed, they were ordered to go back out on the chase immediately and not to return without Dolek. The entire force was mobilized for the search.

They turned the whole ghetto upside down, saving the most intensive search for the block of houses where the Markiewiczes lived. There were all kinds of recesses, yards, and gardens where someone could hide. They spent the whole night running around among the houses, prying into every corner with their lanterns. They had to find him. They had to make up for the ignominy they had incurred in permitting a lone prisoner to escape the custody of ten policemen. After they had gotten over their first paroxysms of fear, the policemen now vied with one another to see who would prove the bravest.

Back in the apartment at Number 13, the youths waited with baited breath. Time after time a light flashed through one of the windows, and time after time footsteps approached the building, then retreated. The voices stopped and started. The men outside were so close it seemed they would be on top of them at any moment. The police had known about Number 13 for a long time, and it seemed nothing could be simpler for them than to walk in and take the whole lot.

Yet they didn't enter. They passed up the opportunity to break into that familiar house, a house they knew was often suspiciously full of young people. How to explain it? Really, it was inexplicable.

Maybe they were still reeling from Dolek's escape. In the confusion, they acted incompetently. They shone their lights into the windows at least a hundred times without once seeing anything to arouse their suspicions. Fear had put blinders over their eyes. At dawn the footsteps quieted down and the police left. The youths inside remained on the alert for another hour. Maybe the police would return. But everything remained quiet. They were no longer under surveillance.

Night was almost over. It was time to get up and dress, but no one moved. No one hurried to get out of bed, though they were in danger and though there was nothing to detain them, since life at Number 13 had lost its charm. Still, they did not want to leave this place, the last home they would ever know. These were the last minutes they were to spend under their own roof, the last minutes these loving companions would share as a cohesive group.

As the first rays of daybreak stole through the windowpanes, they slowly began to rise from their beds. A new day had arrived—a gloomy, dreary day.

Epilogue

-+->-<+-

THERE WAS NOT a single person in the movement who didn't spend at least one evening at Jozefinska 13 — with one exception. That exception was Justyna. She alone was not privileged to imbibe warmth and sustenance from the spiritual treasures of that apartment, where the hours arranged themselves in a brilliant mosaic. Each one who dipped a cup into those living waters drew it out filled to the brim. They poured all the riches of their souls into that limpid pool, and all drank of it in equal measure. Everyone left some memento behind, some spark to be remembered forever: a haunting thought spoken impulsively, a melody beautifully sung, a witticism that inspired a spontaneous outburst of laughter. They gave all they possessed so that together they could construct their beautiful communal life.

[HERE THE DIARY BREAKS OFF.]

APPENDIX

The Akiba Pledge

+>-<+

I PLEDGE to engage in active resistance within the framework of the Jewish Fighting Organization of the Halutz Youth Movement.

I swear by everything most dear to me, and above all by the memory and honor of dying Polish Jewry, that I will fight with all the weapons available to me until the last moment of my life to resist the Germans, the National Socialists, and those in league with them, the mighty enemies of the Jewish people and of all humanity.

I pledge to avenge the innocent deaths of millions of children, mothers, fathers, and aged Jewish people, to uphold Jewish spirit, and to raise the flag of freedom proudly. I pledge to shed my own blood fighting to achieve a bright and independent future for the Jewish nation.

I pledge to fight for justice, freedom, and the right of all human beings to live in dignity. I will fight side by side with those who share my desire for a free and equitable social order. I will serve humanity faithfully, dedicating myself without hesitation to achieving human rights for all, subordinating my personal desires and ambitions to that noble cause.

I pledge to accept as a brother anyone willing to join me in this struggle against the enemy. I pledge to set the seal of death on anyone who betrays our shared ideals. I pledge to hold out to the end, not to retreat in the face of overwhelming adversity or even death.

References and Related Readings

-->-<-

Ainsztein, Reuben. *Jewish Resistance in Nazi-Occupied Europe: With a Historical Survey of the Jew as Fighter and Soldier in the Diaspora*. New York: Barnes and Noble, 1974.

Bauminger, Arieh L. *The Fighters of the Cracow Ghetto*. Jerusalem: Keter Press, 1986.

Browning, Christopher. *Ordinary Men: Reserve Police Battalion 101 and the Final Solution in Poland*. New York: Harper Perennial, 1993.

Dawidowicz, Lucy. *A Holocaust Reader*. New York: Behrman House, 1976.

Dear, I. C. B., ed. *The Oxford Companion to World War II*. New York: Oxford University Press, 1995.

Draenger, Gusta Davidson. *Yomanah shel Yustina* (Hebrew). Translator unknown. Tel Aviv: Beit Lohamei Haghetaot Vehotsaat Ha-Kibbutz ha-Me'uhad, 1952 or 1953; 2nd ed., Introduction by Nachman Blumental. Tel Aviv: Beit Lohamei Haghetaot Vehotsaat Ha-Kibbutz ha-Me'uhad, 1977.

Edelman, Marek. *The Ghetto Fights*. New York: General Jewish Workers Union of Poland, 1946.

Friedman, Philip. *Roads to Extinction*. Edited by Ada June Friedman. New York: Jewish Publication Society, 1980, 333–80.

Graf, Malvina. *The Krakow Ghetto and the Plaszow Camp Remembered*. Tallahassee: Florida State University Press, 1989.

Gutman, Yisrael. "Youth Movements." In *Encyclopedia of the Holocaust*. 4 vols. New York: Macmillan, 1990, 4:1698.

———. *Resistance*. New York: Houghton Mifflin, 1994.

Kaplan, Chaim A. *Scroll of Agony: The Warsaw Diary of Chaim A. Kaplan*. Edited and translated by Abraham I. Katsh. 2nd ed., New York: Collier Books, 1973.

Keneally, Thomas. *Schindler's List*. New York: Simon and Schuster, 1982.

Kligsberg, Moshe. "The Jewish Youth Movement in Interwar Poland" (in Yiddish). In *Studies on Polish Jewry: 1919–1939*. New York: YIVO Institute for Jewish Research, 1974.

Krakowski, Shmuel. *The War of the Doomed: Jewish Armed Resistance in Poland, 1942–1944*. New York: Holmes and Meier, 1984.

Nirensztein, Aaron. "Jewish Resistance in Krakow under the German Occupation" (in Yiddish). Warsaw: *Bleter far Geschikhte (Historical papers)* 1–2 (1952): 226–63.

Pankiewicz, Tadeusz. *The Cracow Ghetto Pharmacy*. Translated by Henry Tilles. New York: Holocaust Library, 1987.

Perlis, Rivka. *The Fighting Pioneers*. Tel Aviv: Ghetto Fighters House, 1984.

——. "The Hechalutz Fighting Resistance in Cracow." In *Dapim*. Edited by Asher Cohen, Yhoyakim Cochavi, and Yoav Gelber. Translated by Carl Alpert. New York: Peter Lang, 1991, 221–53.

Rotem, Simhah (Kazik). *Memoirs of a Warsaw Ghetto Fighter: The Past within Me*. Edited and translated by Barbara Harshav. New Haven: Yale University Press, 1994.

Rufeisen-Schipper, Hela. *Farewell to Mila 18* (in Hebrew). Tel Aviv: Beit Lohamei Haghetaot Vehotsaat Ha-Kibbutz ha-Me'uhad, 1990.

Tec, Nechama. *Defiance: The Bielski Partisans*. New York: Oxford University Press, 1993.

Tenenbaum, Joseph. *Underground: The Story of a People*. New York: Philosophical Library, 1952.

Zuckerman, Yitzhak. *A Surplus of Memory: Chronicle of the Warsaw Ghetto Uprising*. Edited and translated by Barbara Harshav. Berkeley: University of California Press, 1993.

—— and Moshe Bassok, eds. *The Book of the Ghetto Wars* (in Hebrew). Tel Aviv: Ha-Kibbutz ha-Me'uhad, n.d.